The
Kendal
Limestone
Way

A walk from

Skipton to Kendal
via
Malham, Settle, Ingleton, Kirkby Lonsdale and Levens Bridge

John Coppack

First published as an ebook in 2015 by Matador, an imprint of Troubador Publishing Ltd.
This printed first edition is published in 2016 by Follifoot Publishing Limited, The Cottage, Rudding Lane, Follifoot, Harrogate, North Yorkshire HG3 1DQ, England.

Dedicated to

The Yorkshire Dales Millennium Trust, a charitable organisation whose objective is to improve the environmental, social and economic well-being of the Yorkshire Dales.

ISBN 9780956246844

Every reasonable effort has been made to ensure that the information in this publication is accurate and as up-to-date as possible at the time of going to publication. However, over the course of time details change and neither the author nor the publisher can accept any responsibility for any loss, injury or inconvenience experienced by any person or persons whilst using this guidebook. It is recommended to check locally on transport, accommodation and other facilities before undertaking the walk described in this book.

Walking is not an entirely risk-free activity and the reader is strongly urged before undertaking the walk to read carefully the safety information on pages 12 and 13 and to share this information with any walking companion(s). Neither the author nor the publisher can accept responsibility for loss, injury or damage, however occasioned, to any person or persons (including their property) undertaking the walk or any section of it.

A sun-dappled glade above Sizerth Castle in Cumbria with wild garlic and bluebells covering the woodland floor

Contents

Locator Map 1

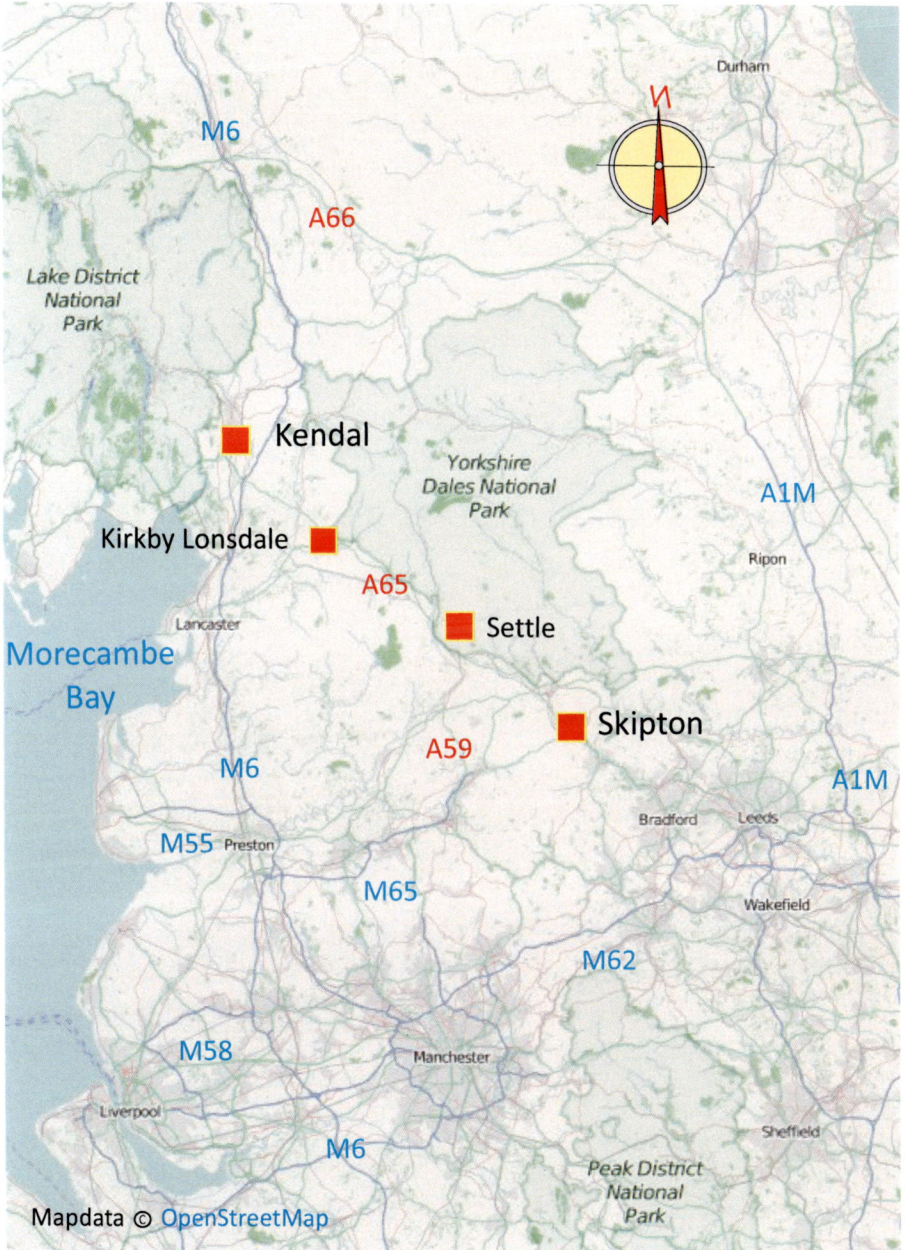

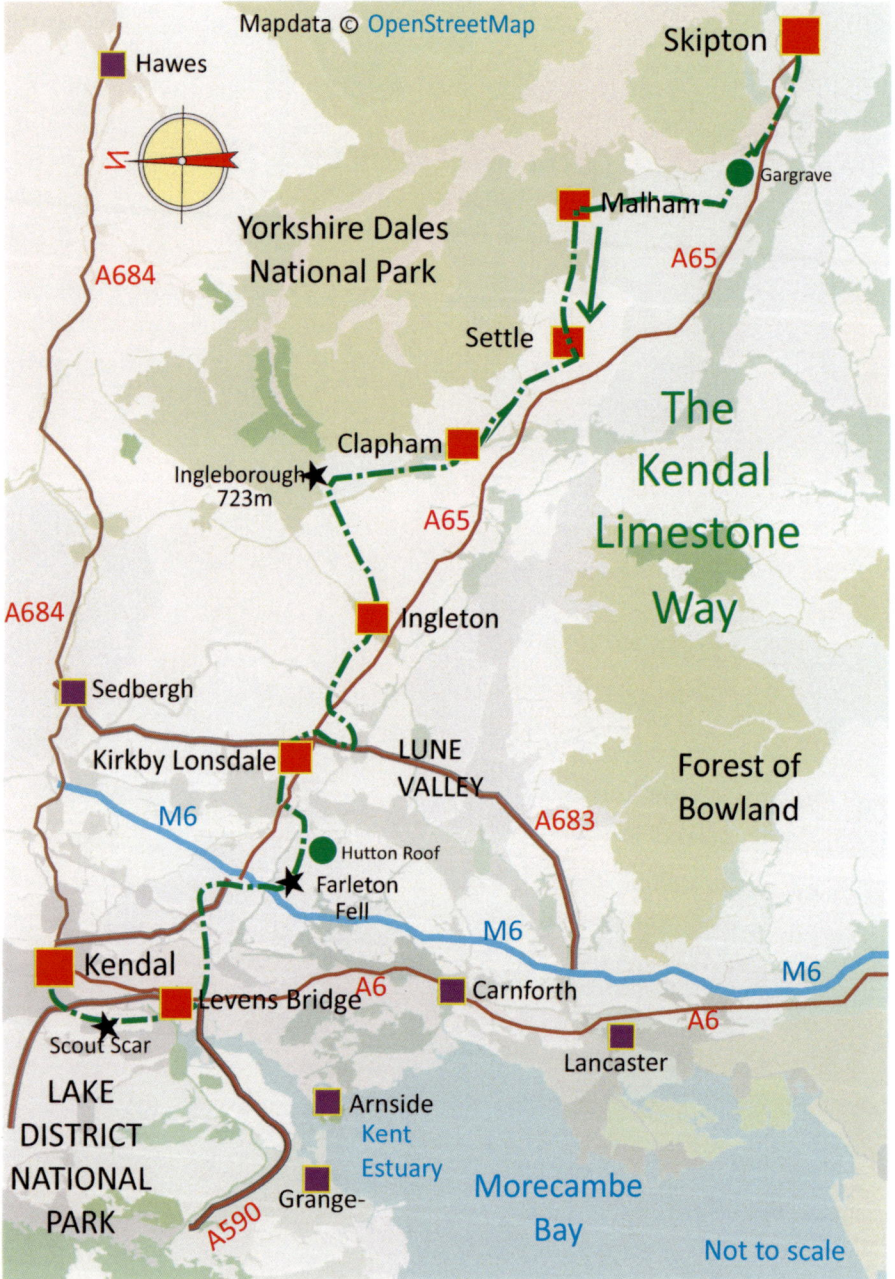

Locator Map 2

Mapdata © OpenStreetMap

Skipton

Hawes

Gargrave

Yorkshire Dales National Park

Malham

A684

A65

Settle

Clapham

Ingleborough 723m

A65

Ingleton

A684

Sedbergh

Kirkby Lonsdale

LUNE VALLEY

A683

The Kendal Limestone Way

Forest of Bowland

M6

Hutton Roof

Farleton Fell

M6

Kendal

Levens Bridge

A6

Carnforth

M6

Scout Scar

A6

Lancaster

LAKE DISTRICT NATIONAL PARK

Arnside

Kent Estuary

A590

Grange-

Morecambe Bay

Not to scale

6

Introduction

The Kendal Limestone Way is the name given by the author to a 63 mile (101km) long linear walk starting from the market town of Skipton in North Yorkshire and ending in the south Lake District town of Kendal. The walk can broadly be divided into three sections. The greater part of the walk is through the limestone country of the Yorkshire Dales National Park. The second, and shortest, section crosses the lower Lune Valley between Lancashire and Cumbria. The final section visits the limestone area to the east of Morecambe Bay, the lower Kent Valley and the south-eastern tip of the Lake District National Park.

The route is almost entirely along field, woodland and riverside paths, canal towpaths, ancient tracks and bridleways and quiet country lanes. An average walker should be able to complete the walk within five or six days. Some people may prefer to complete the walk over a longer period of time, weeks or even months, by completing individual sections as and when the opportunity arises. On the other hand a strong walker could easily complete the entire walk within two or three days.

The main theme of the walk is limestone. Millions of years ago major earthquakes shook the northern Pennines creating massive geological faults and fractures along the southern fringe of the Yorkshire Dales National Park and the south-eastern corner of Cumbria. To the south of the main fault lines lies a large area of millstone grit moorland characterised by the rounded hills of the Bowland Forest in the west and the *Bronte* moors in the east. North of the fault line lie the porous limestone uplands of the Yorkshire Dales National Park where the hills are higher, steeper and more rugged with towering cliffs of pearl white limestone. A limestone landscape is also present in the far south-eastern corner of Cumbria where precipitous limestone ridges form a barrier between the Lakeland hills and Morecambe Bay. The route taken by the Kendal Limestone Way explores this remarkable limestone landscape of northern England.

Accommodation

In devising and plotting the route the author's overriding objective was to start and end each of the seven sections of the walk in a town or village with overnight accommodation. Thus accommodation can be found in Skipton, Malham, Settle, Clapham, Ingleton, Kirkby Lonsdale, Levens and Kendal. Additional accommodation can also be found in the following villages and hamlets which are either en route or close to the route: Gargrave, Giggleswick, Austwick, Lupton, Crooklands and Sizergh.

Terrain

Whilst the raison d'etre for the walk is limestone and much of the route passes through the limestone uplands of the Yorkshire Dales National Park and along the limestone escarpments lying between Morecambe Bay and the Lakeland mountains the route is not entirely over upland fells and hills.

There are three sections where the route crosses relatively low lying terrain. The first of these is between Skipton and Gargrave where the route follows the Leeds and Liverpool canal as it heads towards the rolling hills of Malhamdale. The second is where the route crosses the lower Lune Valley between the borders of Lancashire and Cumbria. The third section is between Farleton in Cumbria and the lower Kent Valley south of Kendal where the M6 motorway, the main west coast railway line and the Lancaster Canal all converge on a narrow strip of coastal plain.

Introduction

Topography

It should be noted that the walk does not take the most direct route to Kendal, either off-road or as the crow flies. One reason for this has already been mentioned, namely the route has been plotted around overnight accommodation. The second reason is that the grain of the land over which the route traverses (ie. glaciated valleys, watercourses and fell ridges) is aligned on an approximate north-south orientation, whereas the route follows a north-westerly course, thus cutting across the grain. Rights of way paths and bridleways generally follow the grain or contour around the grain as this affords the line of least resistance and consequently is less demanding on travellers. On encountering natural obstacles the route invariably zigzags around the obstruction and this increases the overall length of the walk. The third reason is the geographical location of Kendal which lies seven miles from Lake Windermere and less than one mile outside the Lake District National Park. Rising above the town on its western edge is a magnificent mile-long limestone escarpment known locally as Scout Scar. The panoramic views to the Lakeland mountains, the Pennine hills and the Kent Estuary from the plateau are breathtaking and provide a fitting climax to the walk. The inclusion of Scout Scar in the route extends the walk by several miles.

The following is a brief description of the route taken by the Kendal Limestone Way.

Skipton to Malham

From the historic market town of Skipton with its ancient castle, the route follows the Leeds and Liverpool canal to Gargrave where the Romans built a ford across the River Aire. From Gargrave the route takes a north-westerly course along the Pennine Way towards Malhamdale passing close to Airton from where it follows the infant River Aire upstream to Kirkby Malham and its sister village, Hanlith. From Hanlith the route adopts a higher course above the Aire until it reaches the pretty and popular village of Malham, internationally renowned for its dramatic limestone scenery and the Yorkshire Dales "Big Three": Malham Cove, Gordale Scar and Malham Tarn.

Malham to Settle

From Malham the route advances towards a steep pass between Kirkby Fell and Pikedaw Hill. Above the pass the route joins a high level medieval track leading to Nappa Cross Gate and the watershed between Malhamdale and Ribblesdale. After crossing the watershed the route follows the mid-Craven fault that runs below the northern flank of Rye Loaf Hill. After entering Stockdale, a secluded side-valley of Ribblesdale, the route veers away towards the magnificent limestone escarpments of Attermire and Warrendale Knotts before a steep descent into Ribblesdale to join a path leading to the busy market town of Settle nestling under the imposing Castlebergh Rock.

Settle to Clapham

From the Settle, which prides itself on being the "capital" of Ribblesdale, the route crosses the River Ribble and skirts around the picturesque village of Giggleswick, famous for its public school and eye-catching copper-domed chapel, where it joins a rising path leading to the edge of the cavernous but now eerily silent Giggleswick Quarry. From the quarry the route makes a high-level traverse of

Introduction

Giggleswick Scar before descending amongst breathing limestone scenery to the farming hamlet of Feizor and its charming little water-splash. From Feizor the route sets a course for the village of Austwick which it enters via an ancient clapper bridge situated at the foot of Crummackdale.

From Austwick the route follows an ancient walled track that runs below Norber Fell, famed for its limestone erratics, to the village of Clapham which it enters via two tunnels built below the private grounds of Ingleborough Hall.

Clapham to Ingleton

From Clapham, a charming village set in beautiful woodland and bisected by an exquisite beck, the route begins what is unquestionably the most challenging section of the Kendal Limestone Way: an ascent of the second highest and most climbed mountain in Yorkshire, Ingleborough via Gaping Gill. From the village centre the route follows Clapham Beck upstream through the private grounds of Ingleborough Hall towards Ingleborough Cave. From the show-cave the route enters Trow Gill, a dry overhanging ravine, before emerging onto semi-open moorland where a path leads to Gapping Gill, a nightmarish hole in the ground that devours the entire contents of Fell Beck whose waters plunge 96m into a huge chasm large enough to accommodate York Minister. From Gapping Gill the route strikes out for a subsidiary ridge of the main mountain known as Little Ingleborough from where a path leads onto the summit plateau which provides panoramic views to the Lakeland fells, Morecambe Bay, the Wenning Valley, Ingleborough's two companion fells, Penyghent and Whernside, and the Ribblehead Viaduct. From the plateau a rough mountain path falls steeply away towards lower ground above Crina Bottom farm on the Ingleton side of the mountain. Beyond the farm the route joins a green lane which morphs into a footpath over open ground above the village of Ingleton.

Ingleton to Kirkby Lonsdale

The route leaves Ingleton, a village at the confluence of the rivers Twiss and Doe, and famed for its glens and waterfalls, show-cave and spectacular scenery, for Scar End where it makes a left turn to briefly enter Kingsdale, a classic limestone dale, before climbing out of the valley on a steeply rising path that threads its way through huge blocks of limestone to join an ancient high-level track leading to the farming settlement of Masongill. Beyond Masongill the route enters the attractive village of Ireby situated at the foot of Ireby Fell. The border with Lancashire is crossed as the route presses on towards the villages of Leck and Cowan Bridge where four of the Bronte sisters attended school. From Cowan Bridge, the route follows Leck Beck downstream before setting a course for Kirkby Lonsdale where the Kendal Limestone Way enters Cumbria via a remarkable three-arched, 15th-century bridge (known locally as *Devil's Bridge*) spanning the River Lune.

Kirkby Lonsdale to Levens Bridge

From the elegant and prosperous market town of Kirkby Lonsdale situated above a bend in the River Lune the route passes through the settlements of Low and High Biggins before adopting the Limestone Link footpath to Hutton Roof, a village lying under the eastern lee of Hutton Roof Crags. On a steeply rising path that threads its way between outcrops of limestone the route joins a balcony linking Hutton Roof Crags with neighbouring Farleton Fell.

Introduction

Along this section of the route three counties generously contribute to the scenic qualities of the landscape. Cumbria's contribution includes the blue-tinted Howgills, the Middleton Fells beyond Kirkby Lonsdale, a skyline of rolling Lakeland tops and verdant Scout Hill rising above Lupton Beck. Lancashire donates its lonely outpost, Leck Fell, and Yorkshire bestows its famous landmark, Ingleborough along with its satellite hills.

The route contours around the western flank of Farleton Fell above the tiny settlement of Newbiggin. On reaching Farleton, a hamlet a mere five miles from the shores of Morecambe Bay, the route joins the towpath of the Lancaster Canal which it follows northwards passing underneath the M6 motorway and through Crooklands, a village straddling the A65 and the home of the Westmorland County Show. The route from Crooklands to Stainton Bridge, the terminus of the watered section of the canal, is a joy to behold. Here the canal takes on the appearance of a slow, meandering, reed festooned river richly inhabited by various species of waterfowl. Beyond Stainton Bridge the route passes below the busy A590 and the main west coast railway line between London and Scotland as it progresses towards Hincaster and its eponymous canal tunnel, now sadly redundant. From the entrance of the tunnel the route takes an overland course to Hincaster Hall before setting a course for Levens Bridge where in front of Levens Hall, famed worldwide for its magnificent topiary garden, the penultimate section of the Kendal Limestone Way comes to rest.

Levens Bridge to Kendal

The final leg of the walk to Kendal starts from Levens Bridge where the route crosses the River Kent which it initially follows upstream through the deer park of Levens Hall. Beyond the deer park the route crosses the busy A590 en route to Sizergh Castle, owned by the National Trust. The Kendal Limestone Way passes in front of the castle as it advances uphill towards Helsington Church built on the edge of an escarpment overlooking the Lyth Valley with the Coniston fells rising in the west.

From Helsington Church the route crosses the Brigsteer Road and on a gently rising path ascends Underwood Scar (which the locals refer to as Scout Scar), a mile-long limestone escarpment providing superlative long-range views to the Lakeland fells, the Pennine hills and the Kent Estuary. After crossing Underbarrow Road the route presses on towards a cairn at the northern tip of Cunswick Scar, a viewpoint with stunning views towards the head of the Kent Valley. From the cairn the route falls away towards the Kendal bypass which is crossed via a footbridge. A rising path leads to the northern perimeter of Kendal Golf Course and after crossing the fairways a downward slopping path is joined providing a splendid bird's eye view of the "Auld Grey Town" sprawling across Kent Valley below. After emerging from Serpentine Wood the route makes a final descent into Kendal passing the Victorian Town Hall where the late and great Alfred Wainwright fulfilled his daytime job as Treasurer to the Borough Council whilst wistfully dreaming of his beloved Lakeland fells. The Kendal Limestone Way terminates below the medieval tower of the parish church in the old township of Kirkland.

Using this Guide

Information panels

This guidebook divides the route into seven sections broadly equating to areas sharing similar physical characteristics, although there is a degree of overlap. The longest section is 11.5 miles (18.5km) and the shortest 5.7 miles (9.17km). Each section is introduced by an information panel showing its distance, the approximate time to complete the section (though clearly this will depend on frequency of stops, level of fitness and prevailing weather conditions), the nature of the terrain, the degree of difficulty (the latter is necessarily subjective for what one person considers to be a strenuous section, another with experience of walking high-level trails in mountainous regions of the world such as the Himalayas or the Alps may find it easy), a brief description of the route, and the relevant OS 1:25 000 map(s) covering the section.

The information panel also includes facilities along the route, ie accommodation, shops, post offices, chemists, public-houses, restaurants, cafes and tea-rooms.

Route directions

To facilitate navigation each section provides a detailed description of the route supported in Appendix A by twenty-five route maps. These maps are based on map data available under the Open Database Licence (www.openstreetmap.org/copyright). The Open Street Map data has been overlaid and supplemented with drawings and information created by the author to highlight the route. However, the reader should always bear in mind that the directions and route maps (which are not always to scale and lack detail such as field boundaries and contours) will be of little use in fog, heavy mist, low cloud or driving snow, where you cannot see more than a few metres ahead let alone a stile in the far corner of a field or an isolated barn or a plantation of trees in the middle distance. Therefore a compass and the relevant OS 1:25 000 map (and a knowledge of their use) are essential items. On the higher sections of the walk you may need to consider an escape route in the event of being overtaken by inclement weather and in these circumstances the relevant OS 1:25 000 map will be essential. It should also be recognised that landmarks change over time. Farms, and all too frequently barns, are converted into residential dwellings, hedges uprooted, trees felled, old stiles replaced by metal gates, walls demolished, rights of way diverted.

Digital Mapping and Global Positioning System (GPS)

Since the publication of the author's previous guidebook, *The Richmond Way,* the digital revolution continues apace and a whole industry has grown up in offering walkers downloadable GPS files to supplement printed maps and guidebooks. For many walkers GPS enabled devices are de rigueur these days. GPS is the cornerstone supporting digital mapping navigation systems and is excellent at tracking distances or finding your location whatever the weather. However, in order to get a good reading you need to be clear of trees and buildings.

If you use the GPS system on your smartphone it will run down your battery very quickly. The handheld dedicated GPS systems have a longer battery life. Whilst these devices are fun to use and in certain situations could be life-saving they are all dependent on battery life and/or the ability to recharge batteries en route and are no substitute for a printed OS map and compass.

Heritage and historical setting

Apart from magnificent scenery, the Kendal Limestone Way is rich in archaeological sites, ancient monuments, prehistoric fields and settlements, ancient tracks and roads, medieval castles, pele towers, fortified mansions, historic churches, manor houses, turnpike roads, 18th-century canals. These historical features of the landscape add an interesting dimension to the walk and are highlighted throughout this guidebook. Each section also provides historical background information on towns and villages en route to Kendal.

Geology of Limestone Country

Whilst it is outside the scope of this guidebook to provide anything but a brief description of the main geological features found in limestone country the reader may find the information in Appendix B adds to the enjoyment of the walk.

Safety Information

Weather and equipment

If the route of the Kendal Limestone Way was transplanted to North America at the same latitude the walker would find him-or herself at least a thousand miles north of New York. In fact, the southern tip of Alaska lies on the same latitude as the walk! Of course, thanks to the Gulf Stream warming the seas around our island, Britain has a breezy, temperate climate. But away from the coast and with even quite modest increases in altitude, the weather conditions can be extremely changeable both in summer and winter. Even in early spring or late autumn it is not uncommon to experience on the fells (and not infrequently at lower levels) raw, damp, cold days with a penetrating wind and temperatures close to or below freezing point.

Several sections of the route are over exposed moors and mountain fells and hills and walkers should be aware of the physical challenges these may present particularly during adverse weather conditions.

The more exposed areas of the route, namely Malham to Settle, Settle to Feizor via Giggleswick Scar, Clapham to Ingleton via Ingleborough, and Hutton Roof to Farleton should not be undertaken by inexperienced fell walkers in winter, early spring or late autumn. The walk to the summit of Ingleborough should not be undertaken by inexperienced fell walkers in adverse weather conditions *at any time of year.* In mist and adverse weather conditions the summit plateau of Ingleborough can be disorienting. It is essential a compass is carried in order to correctly locate the path from the edge of the plateau to Ingleton via Crina Bottom. An alternative low-level route from Clapham to Ingleton avoiding Ingleborough is included in the narrative.

All walkers should be properly equipped with waterproofs, warm clothing, appropriate headgear (winter for warmth and summer for shade) and a good pair of walking boots suitable for the fells. Walkers should carry with them liquid refreshment (in summer dehydration can present a serious danger) and emergency rations, a first-aid kit, a high-factor sun cream, a torch, a whistle, a lightweight survival bag, a mobile phone, although there are black spots along the route, a watch, a compass and the relevant OS 1:25 000 map.

Always check the weather forecast before setting out, but above all know your limitations and be prepared to turn back should the weather deteriorate.

Sink holes, shake holes and pot holes, disused mine shafts and peat hags

All the above are a common feature of the Yorkshire Dales and the Leck Fell area of Lancashire particularly the upland limestone areas. Holes in the ground are potentially dangerous and even a cursory investigation of them is not advised. Unfenced disused mine shafts present a potential danger between Malham and Stockdale. In these areas, especially, do not stray from the designated route (or other rights of way), keep dogs under control, and at all times watch where you place your feet!

Livestock

There are very few areas along the route where you will not encounter livestock, mainly sheep and cattle. Wherever cattle are present there are added risks to the walker owing to their size and weight. In the presence of cattle keep dogs on a lead unless you are in imminent danger of attack in which event let your dog run free. Be extra vigilant in the presence of cows with calves. Never come between a cow and her calf. Dairy cattle (unless with calves) generally are more docile than beef cattle. In the presence of all cattle remain calm but always watchful. Crossing a pasture containing cattle, when there is thunder in the vicinity, is potentially dangerous. Be extra vigilant in the presence of Limousins. If you are unfamiliar with this breed of cattle look it up on the internet. Limousins are very muscular and have a reputation for excitability and can be dangerous.

Bulls are another potential risk although possibly not as great as cows, particularly cows with calves. Statistically, cows injure about three times more people than bulls. The law relating to the keeping of bulls in fields crossed by public rights of way is anything but straightforward. By law farmers must not place dairy bulls over 10 months old in a field crossed by a public right of way. But they can put any other breed over 10 months old in the field provided it is accompanied by cows or heifers and provided the bull does not have a temperamental disposition! No one in their right mind is going to investigate whether the bull in the far corner of the field is one of the permitted exceptions. Just give the animal a wide berth. Incidentally, when a bull has been taken from a field signs denoting its presence should be removed or securely covered. There are landowners who observe this requirement but there are others who do not in the belief that the notice will dissuade walkers from lawfully crossing their land. If you encounter this problem report the matter to the local Rights of Way Office.

Skipton to Malham

Distance: 11 miles (17.7km).

Walking Time: 6 hours approximately.

Terrain: Easy walking throughout the route mainly alongside watercourses and over undulating grazing pastures. Care should be taken on riverside and canal paths particularly after rain where exposed tree roots present a potential hazard.

Waymarking: Reasonably good throughout the route although the Pennine Way section is not as well waymarked as one would expect for a National Trail.

Map: 1:25 000 OS Explorer OL2 - Yorkshire Dales Southern & Western areas

A brief description of the route

From the historic market town of Skipton with its ancient castle the route follows the Leeds and Liverpool canal to Gargrave where the Romans built a ford across the River Aire. From Gargrave the route takes a north-westerly course along the Pennine Way towards Malhamdale passing close to Airton from where it follows the infant River Aire upstream to Kirkby Malham and its sister village, Hanlith. From Hanlith the route takes a higher course above the river until it reaches the pretty and popular village of Malham internationally famous for its dramatic limestone scenery and the Yorkshire Dales "Big Three", namely Malham Cove, Gordale Scar and Malham Tarn.

Accommodation: Skipton offers a good selection of hotels to suit most budgets including inns with rooms, guest houses and B&Bs. Gargrave offers a budget price hotel. Malham has a varied range of accommodation from hotels, guest houses, B&Bs, YHA (hostel), bunk-style accommodation and camping sites. Airton offers a country house hotel as well as a guest house.

Cafes, restaurants and tea-rooms: Skipton has an excellent selection of eateries. Gargrave and Malham have a number of tea-rooms popular with Pennine Way walkers.

Public Houses: Skipton, Gargrave, Kirkby Malham and Malham.

Tourist Information Centre: Skipton.

Yorkshire Dales National Park Centre: Malham.

Post Offices: Skipton, Gargrave and Malham.

Chemists: Skipton.

Village Shops: Gargrave and Malham.

Skipton to Malham

Public Toilets: Skipton, Gargrave and Malham.

Rail Services.   Skipton and Gargrave with services to Leeds, Settle, Giggleswick, Clapham, Lancaster, Morecambe and Carlisle.

Bus Services: Skipton Bus Station with services to Keighley, Harrogate, Grassington, Ilkley, Otley, Leeds, Burnley, Clitheroe and Preston.

National Express operate services to and from Skipton.

The Craven Connection operates a regular bus service to Kirkby Lonsdale via Gargrave, Long Preston, Settle and Ingleton.

Skipton

The market town of Skipton is located within the south-west corner of Yorkshire, a mere two miles outside the Yorkshire Dales National Park, on the course of the River Aire. Its close proximity to the National Park gives rise to the self-proclaimed appellation "Gateway to the Dales". The town lies at the eastern end of the Aire Gap, a broad geological depression which divides the Pennines into two sections - north and south. Over the centuries this natural low-altitude feature has been exploited by road, rail and canal engineers alike for it has placed Skipton at the cross-roads of several major trans-Pennine routes. The A65 from Leeds to the Lake District and the A59 from York to the Wirral peninsula via Liverpool cross at Skipton. The Leeds and Liverpool canal passes through the centre of the town and train services connecting the west coast towns of Morecambe, Lancaster and Carlisle with the major towns and cities of West Yorkshire call at Skipton.

To the north of Skipton are the limestone uplands of the Yorkshire Dales National Park and to the south the millstone grit moors characterised by the Bronte sisters in their novels. Heather capped moorlands with wooded lower slopes fall away into the lower valley of the Wharfe on its eastern edge; and westwards the Craven fertile lowlands, drained by the rivers Aire and Ribble, merge into the rolling hills of the Bowland Forest.

Skipton's popular outdoor market held four days a week

Historic Skipton

The origins of Skipton can be traced to an Anglo-Danish settlement named "Scipton" which in old English means "sheep farm". From the 11th-century the history of Skipton is inextricably linked to its famous castle and the Clifford family.

Skipton Castle

Skipton Castle is the pre-eminent building in Skipton and one of the most complete and best preserved medieval castles in England. The castle, which has been reincarnated on a number of occasions, was hastily constructed as a motte-and-bailey in 1090 (circa) by Robert de Romily, a Norman baron, on land granted by William II. The original wooden structure was rebuilt in stone to withstand Scottish raiding parties in the 12th and 13th-centuries. Between 1310 and 1314 the castle was extensively reconstructed by

Robert de Clifford, a close friend of the king and whose descendants came over with William the Conqueror. The imposing twin-towered gatehouse dates from this period.

War of the Roses

The Cliffords were a pretty battled-hardened family and invariably in the thick of any fighting going on at the time. Two Cliffords, father and son, died supporting the House of Lancaster during the War of the Roses.

Civil War

At the outset of the Civil War the Cliffords, in common with many wealthy land owning northern families, sided with the king against the Parliamentary forces who

The twin-towered gatehouse, Skipton Castle

17

mounted a three-year siege of Skipton Castle. Starvation eventually forced the three hundred brave defenders to surrender to Cromwell in 1645. After the war Parliament ordered the castle be slighted, that is made uninhabitable.

Lady Anne Clifford

Lady Anne Clifford, the last and most famous of the Clifford line, was an extraordinary woman, diarist, patron of the arts, pious, litigious, twice widowed and an energetic restorer of castles and churches and builder of alm houses for the poor.

Lady Anne was born at Skipton Castle in 1590 but brought up in London where at court she was a particular favourite of Queen Elizabeth. On her father's death she was (wrongly) disinherited from his vast Yorkshire estates which stretched almost continuously from Skipton to Penrith in the old county of Westmorland. Lady Anne pursued her claim against her uncle (the main beneficiary under her father's will) and later his son in the Court of Common Pleas.

The litigation dragged on for thirty years. Ultimately, the case was only partially successful but in the event fate intervened and at the age of 59 Lady Anne acquired her rightful inheritance which included a portfolio of six damaged or ruined castles and their estates

With the acquiescence of Oliver Cromwell (surprisingly as the Cliffords were royalists!) Lady Anne set about the restoration of her castles to their former glory often living in each one for many months before moving on in regal-style to the next with her extensive

retinue of servants.

Lady Anne died in 1646.

Industrialisation

The Leeds and Liverpool canal reached Skipton in 1777 and the industrialisation of Skipton took place shortly thereafter. From a sleepy agricultural town there emerged along the banks of the canal wharves, textile mills, warehouses, terrace houses and mill workers' cottages.

This industrial legacy is still evident today although with de-industrialisation many of the old mills have been converted into small business units or residential apartments.

Tourist Centre

Skipton's broad, partly cobbled, tree-lined High Street hosts its famous market which has been held since medieval times. Four days a week, Monday, Wednesday, Friday and Saturday, folk from all corners of Wharfedale, Malhamdale and Airedale and the cities and towns of West Yorkshire converge on the town to shop, meet friends and exchange gossip.

The town is endowed with many independent shops and galleries, tea-rooms and coffee houses, bistros and restaurants.

During the summer months the canal basin is a hive of activity where visitors can hire a boat or take a short trip on a traditional narrow boat or walk along the network of canal towpaths radiating from the basin.

18

The parish church of the Holy Trinity

Church of the Holy Trinity

Holy Trinity Church stands in a commanding position at the top of the High Street. The church, a Grade I listed building, dates from 1300.

It was damaged during the Civil War and restored by Lady Anne Clifford whose father's tomb lies within.

Lightning strikes down the centuries have resulted in further restoration work, notably in 1909 by Austin and Paley.

A bronze sculpture of Fred Trueman who lived at Flasby (Skipton)

19

Our walk to Kendal starts from the parish church of the Holy Trinity located at the head of the High Street. From the church walk down the High Street passing below the triangular limestone War Memorial topped by a bronze figure *Winged Victory*. On your left is the Palladian-style Town Hall housing the Tourist Information Centre and the Craven Museum. On the opposite side of the road stands a large ornately embellished building formerly the Andrew Carnegie public library opened in 1910.

Leading off the High Street are half-secreted alleyways that open out into charming courtyards.

Where the High Street divides take the road on the far right signed *Sheep Street*. This ancient thoroughfare contains several listed buildings and where for hundreds of years sheep were traded.

On reaching the foot of the High Street turn right onto Swadford Street. John Spencer, co-founder of Marks and Spencer, was born in this locality. Walk forward towards Belmont Bridge and after crossing the bridge take the slip road on your right. This leads to the canal embankment whereupon join the towpath and walk towards the canal basin, that is away from Belmont Bridge. Old warehouses, converted into a chandlery, a ticket office and various other businesses, line the opposite bank.

The colourful canal basin is the epicentre of Skipton's canal network and the point where the Springs Branch joins the Leeds and Liverpool. It is also the home of a bronze larger than life statue of the Yorkshire and England cricketer, Fred Truman (1931-2006).

In summer you may have to weave your way through a crowd of strolling tourists, inquisitive locals, narrow boat skippers and crew, mothers with push-chairs and excited children.

Colourful Springs Branch, a spur of the Leeds and Liverpool Canal

Leaving the throng behind continue along the heritage trail as this section of the towpath is officially designated passing old mills that have either been converted or undergoing conversion into luxury apartments. The parkland on your right is Aireville Park which hosts a number of sporting events throughout the year.

One of the pleasures of this section of the walk is to stand and watch the crew of the narrow boats operate the swing bridges.

A little over one mile from the canal basin the towpath passes under the viaduct carrying the road to Halifax and which marks the end of the heritage trail.

Just beyond the viaduct the canal contours below Niffany Hill which bestows its name on a nearby farm and narrow boat moorings along the canal bank. By the farm the towpath comes to an abrupt halt on encountering the A6069 and is replaced by a

The Springs Branch (above) is a spur of the Leeds and Liverpool canal built in 1797 for Lord Thanet who lived in Skipton Castle. The spur is half a mile long and passes below the walls of Skipton Castle. The canal was built to receive limestone from quarries owned by Lord Thanet at the nearby village of Embsay.

short bridleway running parallel to the road before being reunited with the canal bank. Here the canal is joined by the Leeds-Lancaster-Carlisle railway line which just manages to squeeze itself into a narrow corridor of land betwixt road and canal.

The Springs Branch below Skipton Castle

21

Skipton to Malham

Leeds and Liverpool Canal

The Leeds and Liverpool was something of a laggard when it came to trans-Pennine canal construction. The first two trans-Pennine canals to be opened were the Huddersfield Narrow and the Rochdale. But of the three the Leeds and Liverpool is the only one that has never closed.

Construction of the Leeds and Liverpool began in 1770 and was opened in stages. After various changes of route at the planning stage and funding difficulties it was finally completed in 1816. The canal is 127 miles long and passes through 91 locks including the famous Five Lock Rise at Bingley. The highest point of the canal is 487 feet (148m) above sea level which compared with the other two canals mentioned is fairly modest and a testament to the skills of the surveyors who plotted the low-level route through the Pennines.

The broad locks of the Leeds and Liverpool enabled the canal to compete successfully with the arrival of the railways in the 19th-century. The carrying of commercial freight has all but ceased (in its heyday coal was the main cargo) and today the canal is now almost entirely used for the leisure pursuits of boating, cycling, walking and fishing.

Outward bound for Llangollen, Wales

Looming up is another concrete viaduct; this one carries the busy A59 traffic high above the canal. A little way beyond the A59 the canal sets a more northerly course towards Thorlby, a farming settlement of some antiquity sheltering under the southern lee of Flasby Fell on your right.

A short distance beyond the swing bridge at Thorlby the canal is joined by the A65. In the distance the village of Gargrave, our first objective along this section of the walk, is coming into view. On your left the River Aire is unobtrusively meandering down Airedale towards Skipton and the post-industrial towns of West Yorkshire.

Before entering Gargrave the towpath passes under the A65 and emerges at Holme Bridge Lock, a delightful spot where, during the summer months, excited children watch on as the narrow boats negotiate the two hundred and forty year old lock.

Continue forward passing old warehouses on your right. Cross over bridge 171 that carries the road to Eshton. A short distance beyond Eshton locks is bridge 170. This bridge, known as *Higherland*, marks an important turning point in our walk to Kendal.

Unless visiting the village of Gargrave (recommended for its tea-rooms, parish church and riverside setting) in which case turn left but otherwise turn right, cross the bridge and walk forward to the T junction. Forsake the road on your right. Continue forward along Mark House Lane which is bounded by an estate wall on your left. Gargrave House, completed in 1917 and designed by the renowned Scottish Architect, James Dunn, stands behind the

Gargrave

The pleasant village of Gargrave lying on the southern flank of the Craven Dales is cut in two by the River Aire which runs through its centre almost in parallel to the railway line (south of the river) and the Leeds and Liverpool canal (north of the river).

The canal on reaching Gargrave in 1775, transformed a sleepy village into a transport hub. The mantle has long since passed to the busy A65 (originally a turnpike road from Leeds to Kendal) which slices through the village destroying all vestiges of tranquillity reposing amongst the charming old cottages lining the main street.

The village is strategically placed on the Pennine Way and exploits its favourable location by offering hikers welcome refreshments at several cafes and inns.

A signpost alongside the Leeds and Liverpool

There is evidence of small scale Roman occupation on a site south of the village known as Kirk Sink where there once stood a Roman Villa. The site has been excavated but little remains above ground. Below the bridge leading to the parish church there is a paved Roman ford. The original stone sets can be seen when the river is running low

St Andrew's parish church was rebuilt in 1852 but its original perpendicular tower dating back to the 16th-century is still intact. Within the church are fragments of Anglo-Danish crosses from the 9th and 10th-centuries. Ian Macleod (1913-1970), an influential minister in the Macmillan government of the 1950s and early 1960s, is buried in the churchyard.

Stepping Stones, River Aire

wall. The house has been converted into luxury private apartments.

The parkland on your right belonged at one time to Eshton Hall. After a short distance the road morphs into a gently rising single track lane with open fields on your left and a plantation on your right. Ignore the field path on your left.

War Memorial, Gargrave

24

Leave the track on reaching a signpost on your right inscribed *Pennine Way and Airton.* A stone stile leads into a large pasture.

For such a well-promoted National Trail the Pennine Way path is surprisingly amorphous. Initially aim for a gap between a barn on your left and a belt of trees on your right and with luck you should spot a waymark on the right-hand side of a large gate. Pass through the gate and cross the pasture on a left diagonal course aiming for a wood beyond the rise but diverting to a kissing gate (waymarked) 150m or so from the wood. You have reached the summit of Harrows Hill which, though of modest elevation, provides commanding views to the surrounding hills. Over to the west, aligned on a north-south orientation, are a series of smooth rounded hillocks. These are drumlins formed during the final stages of glaciation. On the skyline beyond Gargrave and its conspicuous church the shapely profile of Pendle Hill, forever associated with Lancashire witches, presents a long-distance landmark. Looking eastwards are the sister peaks of Sharp Haw and Rough Haw, which together form part of Flasby Fell, and beyond them are Haw Fell and Cracoe Fell. In the direction of travel the pearl white limestone rocks at the head of Malhamdale provide the main focus of interest.

Cross the next pasture on the same diagonal course aiming for a small wooden gate alongside a wire fence. After the gate, and still maintaining the same line of march, cross the next pasture aiming initially for the left corner of a plantation bounded by a stone wall. Do not cross the wall but follow it towards the field corner where it converges with another wall running up the field. Proceed through a wooden gate set alongside a signpost for the *Pennine Way*.

Once again maintaining the same left diagonal course cross the large pasture - referred to as *Eshton Moor* on the OS maps. The field on your left contains a tumulus or burial mound of the long barrow-type, possibly dating from the late Neolithic period. South of the tumulus is Haw Crag recognisable by its OS trig pillar and at 206m the highest point on this section of the walk. Throstle Nest Farm is over to your right and about one and a half miles ahead lies the village of Airton, our next objective. The conspicuous house in the valley below is Newfield Hall, a 19th-century country house which has been converted into a hotel.

As you advance across the broad sweeping pasture a fingerpost directs to the bottom left-hand corner of the field. On reaching said corner a wooden gate provides access to a green way enclosed by a limestone wall on your left and a wire fence running parallel to Malham road. Go with the limestone wall which leads to a wooden gate above a tributary stream. The path beyond the gate leads to a footbridge crossing what at first glance looks like a classic Dales' beck. The beck is in fact the infant River Aire, one of the major rivers of Yorkshire. Cross the river and proceed through two successive gates. The broad path follows the river upstream through picturesque meadows before funnelling into a single file path as it enters a wood, the floor of which in late spring is carpeted with wild garlic. Exit the wood and rejoin the riverside path which eventually terminates on the left-hand side of Newfield Bridge. A gap stile leads onto the road whereupon turn right, cross the bridge and 50m beyond on the left is a path signed *Airton.* Having switched banks the path, which presents no navigational difficulties, tracks the river upstream through a succession of pleasant riverside meadows.

After three quarters of a mile the path terminates at Airton Bridge. To visit Airton (recommended but no facilities) cross the bridge. The village lies just beyond the brow of the hill.

Our route bypasses the village and continues along the east bank of the Aire towards our next objective, Hanlith.

The mill on the opposite bank was originally a medieval corn mill owned by Bolton Abbey. In 1787 a new "Arkwright" style cotton mill was erected alongside the old mill and in the 19th-century the mill, now under the ownership of the Dewhurst family (of cotton bobbin reels fame), built a new mill which ceased production in 1904.

During World War II the mill was used for

Airton

Airton can trace its history back to the Norman Conquest when it was known as Airtone. Airton, like many Dales' villages, has a strong non-conformist Christian tradition. One of the oldest buildings in the village is the Friends' Meeting House built in 1690 and still used for meetings, retreats and worship.

In keeping with Quaker tradition the village has no pub.

The garage adjacent to the charming cottage standing on the village green was formerly a squatters' cottage where persons of no fixed abode would be offered shelter.

"The Squatters' Cottage", Airton

the production of Dettol disinfectant after the Reckitt's factory in Hull was bombed. The old mill has more recently been given a new lease of life by being converted into residential units.

The route to Hanlith passes through pleasant riverside meadows and the occasional sighting of a wading bird adds to the enjoyment of the walk.

As you approach Hanlith the riverside meadows give way to open parkland. On reaching Hanlith Bridge take the stone steps leading up to a quiet road. For those wishing to visit Kirkby Malham Church (highly recommended) or the village pub turn left and walk forward for 600m. On your immediate right is the driveway to Hanlith Hall and a few paces beyond is Badger Hill. The latter is our route which passes the

The River Aire

The River Aire is one of Yorkshire's major rivers. It springs to life at Aire Head about half a mile below the village of Malham and for the next seventy-one miles flows south-eastwards through Yorkshire (North and West) before disgorging its waters in the River Ouse above the East Yorkshire town of Goole.

Skipton, Keighley, Bingley, Shipley, Leeds and Castleford are the principal towns of the Aire.

attractive hall built in 1892. This is the third building to occupy this site, the original being erected in 1668. The road winds steadily uphill through the hamlet passing former estate cottages that have been

A converted cotton mill alongside the River Aire

Skipton to Malham

Kirkby Malham is the principal village of Malhamdale and was founded by the Danes over a thousand years ago. The village featured in the great Domesday Book Survey of 1086.

The outstanding building in the village is the Grade I listed church dedicated to St Michael the Archangel. The church, built of millstone grit, was founded in the 9th-century but completely rebuilt in the 15th-century with extensive restoration work being carried out in 1879-81 by Paley and Austin.

In Craven the fashion for church design was for long, low squat buildings with a short tower and straight-headed windows. The parish church at Skipton conforms to this design pattern as does the church here at Kirkby Malham.

Inside the church the font dates from the 11th-century and the box-pews from the 17th and 18th-centuries.

For such a small village the church is disproportionately large (often referred to as the "cathedral of the Dales"). The explanation lies in the fact that the parish for which the church serves is not confined to the village but Malhamdale which extends to some thirty-five square miles and includes eight townships.

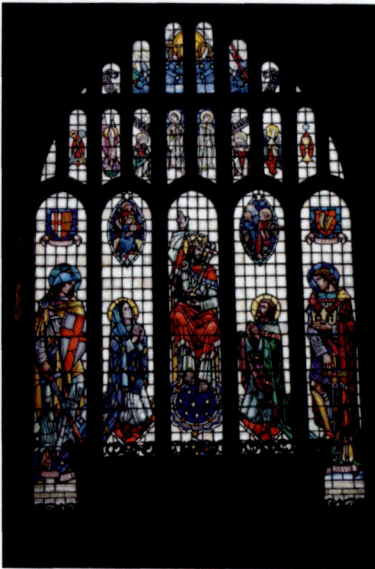

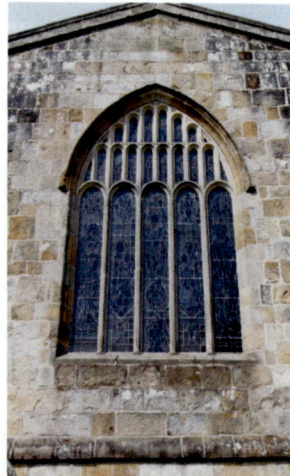

St Michael's Church, Kirkby Malham

"The Cathedral of the Dales", Kirkby Malham

been attractively modernised.

When you reach Flatt House Farm, which is the last dwelling on your left before an acute right-hand bend, pause. On the right of the farm is a signpost for *Malham*. Join the path which runs parallel to the River albeit at a higher elevation than previously.

After about half a mile the path becomes a little more challenging as it crosses a side valley drained by Gordale Beck. A footbridge provides a dry crossing of the beck.

The path eventually joins a well-walked lane. Such is the popularity of the Malham area with walkers twin stiles are a feature of heavily-walked public paths and bridleways. The lane leads directly into Malham.

To complete the first stage of our walk to Kendal cross Malham Beck via one of the two ancient bridges.

An old preaching cross standing in the churchyard at Kirkby Malham

A lovely late 17th-century doorway in Craven Dale built during the joint reign of William and Mary

Skipton to Malham

Malham is undeniably a picturesque village with charming stone farmhouses and cottages bestraddling a lively beck that is crossed by two ancient bridges. Its northern aspect is ringed by a tidal wave of limestone. These intrinsic qualities would be sufficient without more to attract a large influx of visitors to the village but add to the intoxicating mix the National Park's "Big Three", Malham Tarn, Gordale Scar and Malham Cove, all of which lie on its doorstep, and you have a major tourist destination. On public holidays and weekends in summer the sheer number of visitors can completely swamp the little village.

About the 3rd-century BC the Brigantes, a fearsome tribe of Celts, arrived in Malhamdale. Even the mighty Romans were reluctant to take on these Iron Age warriors who lived in their little round huts on Malham Moor.

During the turbulent Dark Ages waves of Angles, Danes and Vikings settled in the area and the remains of their settlements have been found throughout Malhamdale and close to the shores of Malham Tarn.

The defeat of King Harold at the Battle of Hastings in 1066 brought about a major change in the feudal system of land ownership. The old Angle-Saxon governing

Monk Bridge, Malham

class with their large landed estates were swept away and replaced by new rulers loyal to King William. The new king granted to William de Percy, a kinsman and powerful Norman lord, a large slice of northern England including a substantial tract of land to the west of Malham.

The Percy family gifted their land in Malham to the monks of Fountains Abbey whose estate was organised into granges where they grazed, sheep, horses and cows. The shepherds of the Malham sheep-run kept huge flocks of sheep on Malham Moor whose valuable wool was mainly sold to Italian merchants.

Malham

The Lister Arms, Malham built in the 17th-century

Bolton Priory was also a considerable medieval landowner in Malham. The grantor of its land was the powerful Mauleverer family whose descendants came from Normandy. The Bolton estate extended to the east of Malham. The dividing line between the two monastic estates was Malham Beck. For almost four hundred years between the mid-12th-century and the Dissolution land in and around Malham was almost entirely under monastic control.

Ancient Buildings and Bridges

Malham retains many fine old buildings dating back to the 17th-century. The oldest is Hill Top Farm on the Cove Road built in 1617, a classic example of vernacular architecture. The Lister Arms was built in the 17th-century. The elegant Beck Hall by the side of Malham Beck was built in the 18th-century as was the centrally located Buck Inn, a former coaching inn.

Adding to the charm of the village are two ancient stone bridges crossing Malham Beck. Monk Bridge dates from 1636 whilst the even older Wash-Dub Bridge dates from the 16th-century and constructed of limestone slabs placed on stone supports in what is known as a clapper design.

16th-century Wash-Dub Bridge, Malham

Malham to Settle

Distance: 5.7 miles (9.2km)

Walking Time: 4 hours approximately

Terrain: Moderate to strenuous walking over rough fells. The section from Malham to Nappa Cross Gate progressively becomes steeper as it climbs towards the summit of a 500m pass before levelling off where the route crosses the Malhamdale-Ribblesdale watershed. Beyond the watershed walking is fairly easy save for the final section where the route makes a steep descent into Settle.

Map: 1:25 000 OS Explorer OL2 Yorkshire Dales Southern & Western areas

A brief description of the route

From Malham the route advances towards a steep pass between Kirkby Fell and Pikedaw Hill. Above the pass the route joins a high-level medieval track leading to Nappa Cross Gate and the watershed between Malhamdale and Ribblesdale. After crossing the watershed the route follows the mid-Craven fault which runs below the northern flank of Rye Loaf Hill. After entering Stockdale, a secluded side-valley of Ribblesdale, the route veers away towards the magnificent limestone escarpments of Attermire and Warrendale Knotts before a steep descent into Ribblesdale to meet a path leading to the market town of Settle.

Accommodation: Settle and Giggleswick offer a reasonable selection of hotels, inns with rooms, guest houses and B&Bs. There are camping sites close to Settle.

Cafes, restaurants and tea-rooms: Settle has a good selection of eateries and tea-rooms with an acclaimed bakery and café overlooking the market place.

Tourist Information Centre: Settle

Post Office: Settle

Chemists: Settle

Public Toilets: Settle

Rail Services: Settle Station with services to Skipton, Leeds and Carlisle. Giggleswick Station with services to Skipton, Lancaster, Morecambe and Leeds.

Bus Services: Local services to Skipton, Gargrave, Giggleswick, Austwick, Clapham, Cowan Bridge, Ingleton, Kirkby Lonsdale, Airton, Kirkby Malham and Malham.

Malham to Settle

Malham Cove

From the National Park Centre walk into the main body of the village passing on your left the Buck Inn. At the road junction bear left (Cove Road) and walk forward passing first the village hall and then a small estate of bungalows both on your left. Opposite the entrance to Beck Hall take the walled bridleway on your left. Shortly a farm track is joined at the head of the bridleway whereupon turn left and after 50m take the steadily rising track on your right. When you reach the water treatment works pause to drink in (no pun intended) the Malhamdale uplands scenery.

Over to your right the great amphitheatre of limestone cliffs forming Malham Cove is the main focus of interest. On closer examination the cliffs are disappointingly grey in colour rather than pearl white as one might expect in limestone country. This dullness is due to lichens and other fungi lining the rock face promoted by water-action.

Whilst the cove undoubtedly provides the main geological interest it is the field systems on Malham Moor that will excite the interest of archaeologists and historians. The dry stone walls enclosing the rectangular fields were a product of late 18th and early 19th-century Parliamentary Enclosures Acts. These walls were superimposed, but not aligned, over much older arable fields which on closer examination have the appearance of corrugated paper. This is a characteristic of medieval strip cultivation where each holding was ploughed by oxen individually.

A few steps beyond the water treatment works the track forks. Take the branch on your left and continue to a water-splash where a stone slab provides a dry crossing of a tiny stream. Just beyond the stream take the path on your right denoted by a waymarker placed opposite a barn on your left.

Cross the pasture aiming for the right-hand side of an isolated barn on the far side. When you reach the barn you should notice a gate leading into a rough pasture. Once through the gate cross a small stream and head up the pasture on a rightward curving course aiming for an isolated tree. The faint path becomes more defined with progress. Keep well away from the dilapidated wall on your left. The path eventually converges with a wall on your right where a gate leads into another rough pasture with shattered limestone rocks above.

The increasingly steep path is easy to follow and the fine views all around provide an interesting distraction from the gruelling climb up the hillside.

Over to your right is Pikedaw Hill (the summit cairn stands at 463m) and those who embark on the climb to the top (off-route) will on clear days be rewarded with tremendous views over Malhamdale. The hill on your left is Kirkby Fell.

Press on to a stile in a stone wall above. A few steps beyond the stile the path forks. Take the right-hand branch which leads up the fellside. At first the path is sketchy. Ignore the side path leading off to the right. The steep path passes to the left of an outcrop of limestone above and shortly draws level with a cave. Beyond the cave the path improves as it turns towards open moorland before crossing a limestone pavement to meet an ancient track used by the monks peregrinating between Malham grange and their sheep-runs in the Settle area.

On meeting the wide track turn left and pause when you reach a three-way signpost alongside a gate known as Nappa Gate (*gate* is derived from the old Norse word *gata* meaning street or road). The views from this vantage point are superb with Malham Tarn and the limestone scars rising above its dark waters taking centre stage.

Stockdale

Sadly, for the last time on this walk, we bid farewell to lovely Malhamdale as we take the bridleway signed *Stockdale Lane*. This is our route but for those walkers interested in ancient landmarks a mere 200m away (off-route) is Nappa Cross erected eight hundred years ago by the monks to guide them across these exposed moors in inclement weather. To visit the (restored) cross turn right on passing through the gate (signed *Langscar Gate*).

A close encounter!

This area abounds with the remains of grassed-over spoil-heaps and shafts from old mine-workings. In the late 18th-century miners working the copper veins below Pikedaw discovered by accident thick deposits of calamine (a zinc carbonate ore) used in the production of brass. Coal mined on Fountains Fell and converted to coke in special stone built ovens was used to smelt the zinc ore. The smelting process took place close to our path and the processed zinc was transported first to Malham and then by horse and cart to Gargrave for onward transportation via canal barge to Leeds.

The broad green path contours around 500m as it crosses the watershed before embarking on a gradual descent towards Ribblesdale. On your left is the curiously named Rye Loaf Hill.

Stockdale Lane

Attermire Scars and Warrendale Knotts

38

Stockdale Farm
c/f with Alfred Wainwright's drawing of the farm reproduced in his Walks in Limestone Country published in 1970

The valley and its surrounding hills above are of considerable geological interest and a textbook example of the mid-Craven Fault. The more rounded hills on the south side of the valley, such as Kirkby Fell and Rye Loaf Hill, are primarily formed from millstone grit and shale. On the north side of the fault line the hills are steeper and rockier and formed mainly from limestone. The fault line running through the valley was caused by major earthquakes started millions of years ago.

Tiny streams fed by springs seeping out of the porous fellside criss-cross the path on its descent down the valley towards Stockdale Farm. The busy farm, neat and clean in appearance and surrounded by hay meadows, is surprisingly large with many outbuildings. The path passes some 200m above the farm and terminates at a gate leading onto a surfaced road (Stockdale Lane) accessing the farm.

At this juncture turn right *(signed Pennine Bridleway and Lambert Lane)* and walk forward for 500m until you reach a left-hand bend where Stockdale Lane sweeps away downhill towards upper Settle. On your right a small wooden gate provides access to a large pasture. On the far side of the stone wall is a fingerpost inscribed *Settle*. This is our route but before entering the pasture take stock of the situation. In adverse weather or failing daylight Stockdale Lane provides an escape route into *Settle* (two miles away). If taking this route follow the surfaced road to the first junction, turn right and follow the unclassified road which leads directly to upper Settle.

Cross the pasture on a fairly well-defined if somewhat wet path which shortly leads to a a wooden gate beyond which a notice board erected by the Yorkshire Dales National Park Authority welcomes visitors to the Attermire Scars Nature Reserve. This marks the beginning of one of the finest limestone walks in Britain. As you walk below the immense limestone cliffs let your imagination run wild. These towering limestone scars could well have been lifted from a Hollywood "wild-west" film set.

After passing through a further gate the paths draws up in front of a stepped stile alongside of which a fingerpost demarcates several paths. Ignore the path on the far side of the wall which starts it journey to *High Hill Lane* via Sugar Loaf Hill. Unless visiting Victoria Cave (signed) continue forward to a wooden ladder stile located where two limestone walls collide in the corner of the pasture.

Proceed into the next pasture on a rising path leading to a disappointingly shallow cave. As you approach the cave the path forks. Toss a coin for it matters not a jot which of the two green paths you take as they both merge into one single path just before a metal gate. The path closest to the cliff face is perhaps the more interesting one. As you approach the metal gate divert to a wooden wicket gate beyond which a

a manicured sward gathers momentum as it makes a steep descent towards Settle. In every direction the scenery is of the highest quality. Blua Crags lie over to your right and in the direction of travel lies the Ribble Valley where road, rail and river run in parallel along the broad valley floor.

On Sundays and public holidays in the summer months you might just glimpse a steam train puffing its way up the valley towards Ribblehead Viaduct as it begins its spectacular journey over the high Pennine moors to Carlisle.

The ugly face of Giggleswick Quarry, now eerily silent, on the far side of the river, is the only discordant feature in a landscape of outstanding beauty and interest.

In its final stage over open fell the path is particularly steep and, unless you are a short-cutter in which case hang your head in shame, comes to rest alongside a waymark post. Turn left and proceed through a wooden gate. The path, now enclosed by stone walls, continues its remorseless decent towards Settle via Constitution Hill, a charming corner of old Settle lined by white-washed stone cottages festooned in summer with colourful hanging-baskets.

The second stage of our walk to Kendal ends in the old market square.

Malham to Settle

A summerhouse in old Settle

White-washed cottages in a corner of old Settle

"Flower Pot Festival" - Upper Settle

Settle

Settle lies on the southern fringe of the Yorkshire Dales and is presided over by a guardian-angel in the form of an imposing limestone crag known as Castlebergh Rock which at 91m high shelters the town from the full force of winter gales sweeping down the Ribble Valley.

Geology

The South Craven Fault runs through the town with gritstone rock surfacing to the west and limestone scars to the east. The River Ribble, which rises amongst a vast tract of desolate, water-logged moorland in upper Ribblesdale, flows through the town on its 56 mile journey to the Irish Sea.

History and transport

Settle is the self-proclaimed capital of Ribblesdale and can trace its roots back to pre-conquest days when it was an Anglian settlement. In 1249 Henry III granted a charter for the town to hold a weekly market, a tradition which is still upheld. Tuesday is market day when the square becomes a sea of colourful canopied stalls and the local dialect is all pervasive as folk from all four corners of Ribblesdale shop, meet and exchange gossip.

Until the building of the bypass to the south of the town Settle provided a convenient stop-over for travellers making their way from the towns and cities of West Yorkshire to the Lancashire coast and the Lake District. Before the motor car the numerous coaching inns of the town provided stabling for horses and food and accommodation for travellers.

From earliest of times Settle has been a transport hub for the southern Dales and interest in the comings and goings of travellers continues to this day. A bus pulls into the market square and instantly there is a ripple of excitement amongst the onlookers as passengers alight - a young mother laden with shopping, students transfixed by their smartphones, an elderly couple returning from an outpatients' appointment in Skipton, ramblers with walking sticks poking out of their rucksacks - all are scrutinised with intense interest.

Architecture

The buildings of Settle are a hotchpotch of architectural styles ranging from the arcaded Shambles (formerly slaughter-houses) in the market square, the distinctive French-style Town Hall on the edge of the market square, the Victoria Music Hall in Kirkgate, a Grade II listed building, and the most eccentric building in the Dales, if not the whole of Yorkshire, the 17th-century house known as The Folly, now the Museum of North Craven Life and a Grade I listed building.

Malham to Settle

The industrial revolution only lightly brushed Settle which in the 1700s developed into a small mill town with water-powered cotton spinning mills lining the banks of the Ribble.

Settle's industrial past is long-over and the town has reverted back to its agricultural and hospitality roots.

But where is the naked woman?
(She does exist)

Market Square, Settle

Malham to Settle

Settle - Carlisle Railway

The Settle-Carlisle railway is considered to be one of the most scenic railways in England. The construction of the railway, which began in 1869, was a major engineering achievement. Twelve tunnels, 15 viaducts and numerous cuttings and embankments were built to carry the 72 mile line across high fells and deep valleys.

Thousands of workers, navvies, stonemasons, blacksmiths, carpenters and their wives and children lived in shanty towns close to the construction site. Over 200 workers and their families died during the construction of the railway either from accident or from an outbreak of smallpox.

The raison d'etre for the line was to provide the Midland Railway Company with a main trunk route from London to Scotland to compete with the Great Northern Railway which operated the east coast route via York and the Great North Western Railway which operated the west coast route via Crewe. Until the opening of the Channel Tunnel link it was the last main trunk line to be built in England.

Ribblehead Viaduct (off-route)

Settle to Clapham

Distance: 7 miles (11.3km)

Walking Time: 5 hours approximately

Terrain: Moderate walking from Settle to Feizor and easy from Feizor to Clapham via Austwick. The terrain is predominantly limestone. The path over Giggleswick Scar runs close to precipitous limestone cliffs.

Waymarking: Excellent from start to finish of the route.

Maps: (1)   1:25 000 OS Explorer OL2 Yorkshire Dales Southern & Western areas; and
(2)   1: 25 000 OS Explorer OL41 Forest of Bowland & Ribblesdale

A brief description of the route

From the Settle the route crosses the Ribble and passes above the picturesque village of Giggleswick, famous for its public school and copper-domed chapel, where it joins a rising path leading to the rim of the cavernous but now ghostly silent Giggleswick Quarry. From the quarry the route makes a high level traverse of Giggleswick Scar passing close to Schoolboys' Tower and numerous caves before descending to the farming hamlet of Feizor. From Feizor the route sets a course for the village of Austwick which it enters via an ancient clapper bridge situated at the foot of Crummackdale. From Austwick the route adopts an ancient track running below Robin Proctor Scar and enters Clapham via two Victorian tunnels built below the grounds of Ingleborough Hall.

Accommodation: Giggleswick offers a hotel plus an inn with rooms. Feizor (when last checked) has a b&b farmhouse. Austwick boasts a country house hotel plus a guest house and Clapham offers a selection of accommodation including an inn with rooms, guest houses, b&bs, a bunkhouse and camping close to the village.

Cafes, restaurants and tea-rooms: Feizor has a farmhouse-style tea-room. Austwick has a restaurant within its hotel and Clapham offers a selection of tea-rooms.

Public Houses: Giggleswick, Austwick and Clapham.

Post Offices: Austwick

Village Shops: Giggleswick, Austwick and Clapham.

Toilets: Clapham

Rail Services: Clapham station is one mile from the village with services to Lancaster, Morecambe, Leeds, Skipton, Giggleswick and Gargrave.

From the market square with your back to *Ye Olde Naked Man* café turn left (those of a less sensitive disposition may face the *Naked Man* in which event turn right) and walk forward passing a church on your right and a service station on your left. Proceed under the viaduct carrying the Settle-Carlisle railway and at the cross-roads continue forward crossing the bridge spanning the River Ribble. Ignore the riverside path on your right leading to Stackhouse.

Press on passing the campus of Settle College. Cross-over Stackhouse Lane - users of the right-hand side pavement only - and continue uphill towards the village of Giggleswick.

The Hartshead Hotel lies ahead. On the same side as the hotel you will notice a tiny triangular green upon which stands a seat. The road forks at this point with the left-hand branch leading down the hill towards the village of Giggleswick. Those wishing to visit the attractive village of Giggleswick (recommended) should leave the route at this juncture.

Opposite the small green an estate road bearing the name *The Mains* joins the main road. This is our route. The road is lined with pleasant houses and bungalows built during the inter-war years with more recent infill developments. The magnificent copper-domed chapel belonging to the public school at Giggleswick can be glimpsed between the dwellinghouses on your left.

The road funnels into a surfaced lane which runs below a large guest house with the name of *Woodlands*. The views across the Ribble Valley are pleasant enough although not exceptional, the main interest being the heritage mills at Stackhouse.

The surfaced lane gives way to a rough track immediately beyond a wooden gate. Press on to a metal gate leading onto open fell land. On the far side of the metal gate the broad track winds steadily up the hillside although at one point it loops back on itself. Ignore all side branches.

As height is gained the main scenic interest is provided by Penyghent which at 694m is, surprisingly, only the ninth highest hill in Yorkshire and usually the first to be climbed on *The Three Peaks* Walk. The track morphs into a single file path as it sets a course for the eastern rim of the now defunct and ghostly silent Giggleswick Quarry which is bounded by a wall on your left carrying warning signs of deep excavations. The rim of the quarry is indeed life-threateningly dangerous and children and dogs should be closely controlled.

The limestone wall on your left is replaced by a wire fence but the path is not difficult to follow running as it does between the wire fence and a dilapidated wall on your right. The path eventually turns away from the quarry rim crossing a highly fractured limestone pavement that leads onto the crest of Giggleswick Scar.

Follow the faint path towards a prominent limestone cairn standing about 250m along the crest. As you approach the cairn you should notice a fingerpost directing to a huge pile of stones over to your left. These are the remains of Schoolboys' Tower built in Victorian times on the edge of Giggleswick Scar and the objective of school boys competing in an annual fell race. The views from the crumbling tower are outstanding

Settle to Clapham

Giggleswick

Giggleswick and Settle stand in close proximity to each other only narrowly separated by the River Ribble but the contrast between the two settlements could not be greater, whereas Settle is all hustle and bustle having long ago sold its soul to tourism, Giggleswick exudes an air of restrained artistic and intellectual aloofness. Behind the lovely 17th-century cottage facades with their weathered mullions one imagines the presence of writers, artists and composers diligently and quietly pursuing their calling.

Giggleswick is renowned for its 15th-century public school where in Victorian and Edwardian times the mill-owners of Bradford and the wealthy industrialists of Leeds would send their sons to be educated in the manners and ways of a "gentleman". Nowadays the school is co-educational and takes pupils from all corners of the world.

Dominating the village and the surrounding countryside is the graceful and perfectly proportioned school chapel whose massive copper-domed roof is an iconic landmark for miles around. Its considerable edifice is accentuated by being built on a hillock of gritstone and shale. The chapel was built to commemorate the Diamond Jubilee of Queen Victoria. How fortunate are the residents and students of Giggleswick to have in their midst such an extraordinary fine building set in beautiful grounds.

At the heart of the village stands the splendid 15th-century parish church dedicated to St Alkelda who was a Saxon princess allegedly strangled by Danish invaders in the 12th-century for her Christian faith. The church is a Grade I listed building with traces of pre-Norman conquest stonework.

Next to the church stands an ancient three-stepped market cross although any market held below the cross would have been subsumed long ago into the weekly market held across the river in Settle.

The name Giggleswick is believed to have derived from the personal name of a Scandinavian settler

Giggleswick

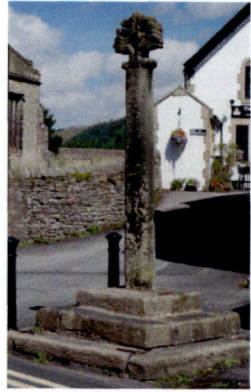

The ancient market cross, Giggleswick

The parish church of St Alkelda, Giggleswick

and merit the short detour off-route. On the skyline beyond the Craven lowlands is Lancashire's famous Pendle Hill. At the foot of the scar is a golf course built on reclaimed land where there once stood a tarn formed from melting ice at the end of the last glaciation. The tarn was drained in 1837 revealing a two thousand year old dug-out boat. The conspicuous copper-domed chapel towering over the public school at Giggleswick attests to its status as an iconic local landmark.

The cliffs of Giggleswick Scar mark the point at which the earth fractured as a result of seismic activity over thousands of years. The relatively flat land below the precipice has slipped below the main fracture line, whereas the cliffs and the limestone uplands to the north stand on land that has been raised upwards by a succession of earthquakes.

Surprisingly, earthquake activity continues to this day for in 1944 (which in geological time is a mere nanosecond away) there was a significant earthquake along the South Craven Fault.

Assuming mother nature has behaved herself and the earth has not opened up below your feet during the time you have been contemplating these weighty geological matters retrace your footsteps to the fingerpost and enjoy the walk along the Scar. No directions are required as the path is easy enough to follow although in poor visibility be careful not to stray from the path as precipitous cliffs fall away on your left-hand side.

The road below the scar was formerly a turnpike and more recently the A65 until the

Settle bypass was built. It has now been relegated to a B road but still bears its old name of Buck How Brow.

A little over half a mile from Schoolboys' Tower the path takes a north-westerly course crossing grazing land before drawing up alongside a signpost demarcating several paths. Ignore the path to Stackhouse and go with the bridleway to Feizor which is our next objective.

With progress the path aligns itself with Yorkshire's most famous mountain, Ingleborough and its attendant hills. In the middle distance the village of Austwick, sheltering under the limestone scars of Moughton and Norber, is revealing its presence. The views from the broad green path winding down towards the farming hamlet of Feizor are simply sublime.

The water-splash at Feizor without water!

49

Feizor

All too soon the path comes to rest alongside a delightful water-splash fed by a tiny tributary stream of Austwick Beck. For those in need of refreshment Feizor has a popular tea-room located a stone's throw away. Turn right for the tea-room which is run by an enterprising local farming family.

Our route to Austwick, our next objective, starts close to the water-splash where a stile leads into a paddock.

(NB There are several routes to Austwick, all delightful, including the *Pennine Bridleway*. The one described in this guidebook leads directly to the northern tip of the village and thus the onward path to Clapham).

A series of stiles, some ladder others stone-stepped, lead from one grazing pasture to another below the southern slopes of Feizor and Oxenber woods. Navigation is straightforward although the stiles are rarely in alignment. The final stile in the series

Feizor (pronounced Fayzr) lies within a mile of the A65, yet most travellers hurtling along this busy highway will be oblivious to the charms of this farming hamlet which once offered hospitality to the monks of Fountains and Sawley abbeys as they made their way to and from their granges in the Lake District.

For hundreds of years, before the coming of the turnpikes, the hamlet was on the old packhorse route between York and Lancaster.

Feizor, a name which has Norse connotations, was formerly a "sheiling" or summer dwelling in the hills where farmers in medieval times took their livestock for summer grazing.

The hamlet stands on the cross-roads of several scenic walking trails.

Feizor

Flascoe Bridge, Austwick

admits to an enclosed footpath running across the direction of travel. On the opposite side of the footpath you will notice a ladder stile. This is not our route. On joining the path turn right and after a short distance pass in front of Wood House Farm which lies below the western slopes of Oxenber Wood.

A little way beyond the farmhouse you reach a junction of paths which are signposted. Go with the *Pennine Bridleway to Austwick*. From the enclosed bridleway the views all around are entrancing but it is Crummackdale with its lush pastures enclosed on three sides by limestone scars that provide the main scenic interest. The narrow lane shortly draws up alongside a

medieval clapper bridge with stone slabs providing a dry crossing of Austwick Beck.

The bridge is called *Flascoe* and on warm summer days young children from the village, under the watchful eye of their guardians, paddle and play in the beck and picnic on the banks above the old ford.

Cross the bridge and follow the path which after 300m joins an unclassified road running through the northern environs of Austwick. Turn left and walk forward for 200m and (unless visiting the attractive village endowed with an elegant Georgian country house hotel and a highly rated pub facing the green) bear right at the first road junction. Walk up the lane which is lined

Robin Proctor Scar

A charming corner of Austwick

The stepped market cross, Austwick

with some of the oldest houses in the district. Town Head Hall (which is open to the public at set times and days of the year) is a former fortified manor house which has undergone many changes down the years.

Forsake the path on your right running between private gardens. A little way beyond the housing on your left is a half-hidden fingerpost inscribed *Clapham*. This is our route. Beyond the stile the path initially hugs the wall on your left before bearing away towards a ladder stile admitting to Thwaite Lane, an ancient monastic highway which after the Dissolution was adopted by drivers of packhorse "trains" for the carrying of coal, iron ore, lead, wool and general merchandise to the tradesmen and farmers of the Dales.

On reaching the lane turn left and head for Clapham. On your right is further evidence of seismic activity along the line of the North Craven Fault. The limestone cliffs of Robin Proctor Scar are the result of these mighty upheavals many years ago.

It is highly unusual in these parts for a geological feature to be named after a local person. Poor Mr Proctor, a local farmer, had the misfortune in poor visibility to ride his horse over the precipice now dedicated to him.

Unfortunately, history does not record whether rider and horse survived the fall.

The ancient track affords an opportunity to do some hill spotting. Over in the north-west lies Ingleborough and its subsidiary summit, Little Ingleborough, which will soon dominate the mid-section of our walk to

Austwick

Austwick is an old Norse settlement whose fortunes have waxed and waned over the centuries. At the time the Royal Commissioners paid their visit in or about 1086 to record its landed assets for the Domesday Book Austwick was the head of an honour comprising twelve manors. In medieval times Austwick held a market as evidenced by the old cross on the green but the market eventually lost its business to a rival at nearby Clapham.

Austwick is the gateway to the Norber boulders, a geological freak of nature. These boulders, or erratics as they are more correctly termed by geologists, are a legacy from the last Ice Age. As the glaciers melted great rocks of Silurian gritstone were swept down the valley floor eventually coming to rest on a bed of limestone which over the centuries has eroded away leaving the alien rocks precariously balanced on narrow stone pedestals.

From the 7th-century onwards Anglo-Saxon farmers ploughed the land to the west and east of Austwick. The ancient strip terraces (or lynchets as they are sometimes called) are still discernible particularly after a dusting of snow.

Kendal. Norber, famed for its erratic boulders, occupies the north-eastern aspect and a little further to the east stand Moughton and Oxenber.

Pendle Hill, in the manner of a benevolent uncle in a family photograph, always manages to slide into every southern view. In the south-west lie the Bowland Fells

Thwaite Lane, Austwick

On a clear day you cannot fail to notice the spinning turbines over in the south-west. The wind farm stands above the village of Caton, close to Lancaster, in a designated area of Outstanding Natural Beauty!

As you advance along the lane you should notice a fingerpost on your right bearing the inscription *Norber ½ mile*. The path provides an interesting detour for those who wish to examine at close quarters the geological freak boulders known as erratics. Unless making the detour continue along the lane passing on your right Long Lane marked by a signpost inscribed *Selside*.

If you had stood at this spot two hundred

and fifty years ago the chances of being run-over by a coach-and-four were fairly high, for Long Lane was on the main trans-Pennine coaching route between Lancaster and Newcastle. Today Long Lane provides an alternative route to the lower slopes of Ingleborough for those walkers who wish to bypass Clapham or avoid the two dank, gloomy tunnels looming up.

In 1833 the owners of Ingleborough Hall extended their property over Thwaite Lane and to preserve the ancient right of way they built two tunnels (actually three but one is blocked up). The first tunnel is the longest and the darkest. Both are dank and care is required as the pathways are wet and slippery. Ideally, both tunnels should be lit but lighting would no doubt detract from the dubious pleasure of stumbling along in the darkness.

Beyond the second tunnel stands the village church dedicated to St James. The third stage of the Kendal Limestone Way terminates in the shadow of the church.

A quiet corner of Clapham

Clapham

There is a certain uniformity of architectural style about the neat and tidy buildings comprising Clapham; they appear to date from the same period. In fact today's Clapham is an estate village built and planned by the local Farrer family in the 1830s.

The pretty village has an ancient pedigree going back to Saxon times. In 1201 Clapham received from the king a charter to hold a market and livestock fairs. The market cross stands near the bridge on the main road but, alas, the market and sheep fairs closed for business a long time ago.

Clapham Beck

55

Two family names are synonymous with
Clapham - Faraday and Farrer. The former
was a blacksmith (etymologically it should
be the reverse) whose son, Michael, became
one of the greatest scientists in history.
There can be few schoolchildren who have
not heard of his pioneering work in
electricity and magnetism.

The second son of Clapham is Reginald
Farrer, the internationally renowned
botanist and plant collector, who before his
untimely death at the age of 40 introduced
many new plants to Britain

Ingleborough Hall was the home of the
Farrer family for nigh on one hundred and
fifty years. Today it is an Outdoor Education
Centre.

Church of St James, Clapham

Clapham Beck

Clapham to Ingleton

Distance: 6.5 miles (10.5 km).

Ascent: 560m

Walking Time: 5 hours approximately.

Terrain: The walk from Clapham to Ingleton via the summit of Ingleborough (elevation from sea level 723m) is by far the most demanding of all the routes described in this guidebook. The route is over exposed mountain terrain and fells and should not be undertaken by inexperienced fell walkers in winter, early spring or late autumn. Even in summer the weather can change suddenly and all walkers should be properly equipped for high-level fell walking. An alternative low-level route to Ingleton is provided in the narrative. The section from Trow Gill to the summit of Little Ingleborough involves a steep ascent and the section from the summit plateau of Ingleborough to Crina Bottom on the Ingleton side of the mountain involves a particularly steep descent.

Waymarking: From Clapham to Trow Gill excellent and from Crina Bottom to Ingleton good. Between Trow Gill and Crina Bottom there are no waymarkers other than cairns which due to their proliferation can be misleading. In mist the summit plateau of Ingleborough can be disorienting. It is essential a compass is carried in order to locate the path from the edge of the plateau to Ingleton via Crina Bottom.

Map: 1:25 000 OS Explorer OL2 Yorkshire Dales Southern & Western areas.

A brief description of the route

From the National Park car park the route follows Clapham Beck upstream through the private grounds of Ingleborough Hall towards Ingleborough Cave. From the show cave the route enters Trow Gill, a dry overhanging ravine, before emerging onto semi-open moorland where a path leads to Gapping Gill. From Gapping Gill the route strikes out for the subsidiary summit known as Little Ingleborough from where a ridge leads onto the main summit plateau. From a large cairn located on the far south-western edge of the plateau a rough rock strewn path falls steeply away towards lower ground above Crina Bottom. Beyond the farm at Crina Bottom the route joins a green lane for a mile and then a footpath over open ground to meet the Ingleton-Hawes road. The village of Ingleton lies half a mile away.

Accommodation: Ingleton offers a traditional hotel, inns with rooms, several guest houses and B&Bs. Ingleton also has a youth hostel. The neighbouring village of Thornton-in-Lonsdale (one mile away) has a 17th-century country inn with modern rooms.

Cafes, restaurants and tea-rooms: Ingleton.

Clapham to Ingleton

Public Toilets: Ingleton

Rail Services: The nearest railway station to Ingleton is at Bentham (4 miles 6.4km away) on the Leeds-Skipton-Lancaster line.

Bus Services: Ingleton is on a local bus network with services to (1) Settle and Skipton (2) Lancaster via Burton-in-Lonsdale and Bentham (3) Kendal via Kirkby Lonsdale and (4) Horton-in-Ribblesdale.

The Craven Connection bus service stops at the village
,

From the National Park Authority car park turn right and then immediately left. Cross-over Clapham Beck and walk up Riverside to a second bridge known locally as *Brokken Bridge*, the name having derived from an earlier structure which was seriously damaged in a disastrous flood in the 1840s.

Continue forward to the Nature Trail which starts inside the grounds of Ingleborough Estate. A ticket is required which for a modest fee is dispensed by a ticket machine at the entrance.

.
For those who have eschewed the charms of the Nature Trail either on the grounds of principle or impoverishment should continue beyond the entrance, take the first right and follow the lane uphill to Clapdale Farm. Just beyond the farm a path on your right leads downhill to rejoin the main route above the private grounds of Ingleborough Hall.

Having collected your ticket enjoy the shaded Nature Trail which follows a broad pathway lined with magnificent beach trees interspersed with fine specimens of ash, chestnut, box and many varieties of conifer all planted above an artificial lake created in the 1830s by the damming of Clapham Beck.

The pathway passes in front a weird-looking Victorian folly known as the grotto.

A metal gate signals the end of the woodland trail.

During school term time you are likely to encounter a conga-like procession of excited and boisterous children making their way to Ingleborough Cave which is the main draw in this part of the Dales

Alternative route to Ingleton in poor visibility

From the National Park car park turn right into Church Avenue and follow the road uphill to the Church of St James. Cross over the bridge and turn right. Walk up Riverside and pause when you reach the Viewing Station for the falls. Ahead is the entrance to the Nature Trail at which point the road bears away from Clapham Beck. Follow the road which, after a short distance, merges into Eggshell Lane. The latter leads to the old road between Ingleton and Clapham via Newby Cote. Stay on this road until you reach Ingleton, a little under four miles away.

The Nature Trail

The Nature Trail is named after Reginald Farrer (1880-1920), a botanist and plant collector of international repute who wandered through Asia collecting exotic plants and trees for botanical gardens such as Kew in London. Many of the specimens brought back to Britain such as azlea, rhododendron and Japanese maple, can be found alongside the Nature Trail. In spring the glades along the trail are ablaze with drifts of bluebells and allium ursinum (wild garlic).

As you advance up Clapdale you pass bunker-like structures built above the beck Those of a curious disposition may wonder what on earth is going on underground. The whole valley echoes to the rhythmic clanking of gasping machinery. The answer to the mystery is underground water-pumps - water extracted from the beck is being pumped to neighbouring Clapdale Farm.

The grassy banks below the ticket office are invariably populated by hordes of children lolling around waiting for the start of the next guided tour through the 550m lighted show-cave.

Having negotiated your way through the throng of enthusiastic young cavers, cross the stone-arched bridge where Fell Beck matures into Clapham Beck

Clapham Beck and proceed up the narrow valley towards Trow Gill, an impressive dry gorge carved out by a once mighty glacial river flowing down the slopes of Ingleborough at the end of the last Ice Age. The name Trow Gill means steep wooded valley and is popular with "zippers".

The head of the gorge narrows considerably and at first sight appears to end in a cul de sac; however, a narrow boulder strewn neck provides a way out. With the constant pounding of boots over the years the boulders have become slippery and a degree of mild scrambling may be called for in order to exit the dank gloom of the neck.

Once into daylight the stony path hugs a limestone wall on your left and continues along the upland dry valley towards open moorland which is accessed via a twin stile. Disregard the path on the opposite side of the stile. Cross the twin stile and follow the path which runs to the right of a large shake-hole known as Disappointment Pot, so named because earlier explorers failed to find a passageway connecting it with the Gapping Gill System.

About 250m beyond the twin stile, the path forks - the narrower of the two paths strikes out for Little Ingleborough and the broader path on the right leads to Gapping Gill "the daddy of them all" in the words of Alfred Wainwright. The Gapping Gill path is our route.

By all means view Gapping Gill from the safety of the perimeter wire fence but to venture to the lip of the main shaft would be extremely foolhardy with possible tragic consequences.

Gaping Gill

Gaping Gill is Britain's second deepest pothole and Fell Beck which disappears down the main shaft is England's highest waterfall. The shaft is 98m long and the main chamber, which would hold York Minster, is 152 x 27 x 34m. Fell Beck re-emerges lower down the valley at Beck Head, a spot close to Ingleborough Cave, having travelled one mile through subterranean channels.

It would be fitting to write that the first person to descend the nightmarish depths of the main shaft was an intrepid Yorkshire man or woman but, alas, that accolade goes to a brave French explorer, Edward Alfred Martel, who in 1895 used a rope ladder to reach the floor of the main chamber. The descent took him twenty-three minutes and the assent a mere five minutes more.

A path on the south side of Gapping Gill rejoins the main path to Little Ingleborough. Erosion of the fellside caused by the multiplicity of paths leading to the summit has led the National Park Authority to construct a stairway (if not quite to heaven)

in the form of huge stepping stones. Nevertheless, the path is exceptionally steep and considerable care is required particularly in wet or icy conditions.

From the summit of Little Ingleborough a clear path leads to the south-eastern corner of the main summit plateau. Cross the plateau to reach the OS triangulation pillar with a toposcope for those with a suitable app on their smartphones to read it.

The path to Ingleton starts from the south-western edge of the plateau, a little to the left of the remains of a former hospice and to the right of a small cairn.

Gapping Gill

Trow Gill

61

The ruins of the hospice are about 100m from the OS triangulation pillar built of stone.

OS trig pillar, Ingleborough

The rock strewn path falls steeply away from the summit plateau towards Crina Bottom. The rough path is well-trodden by walkers and except in exceptional weather conditions presents no navigational problems.

At Crina Bottom the path passes to the left of an isolated farm with a wind-turbine above the house. A short distance beyond the farm a ladder stile admits to a walled green lane (Fell Lane).

Go with the undulating lane. Ignore the path on your right to Skirwith (unless you wish to bypass Ingleton and rejoin the author's route at Twisleton Hall). After about a mile

the lane morphs into a path over semi-open ground as it rapidly descends the lower fell.

On reaching the unclassified road linking Ingleton with Hawes turn left and edge your way down the narrow road taking care as there are no pavements and for 100m you are at the mercy of HGVs and huge tractors towing an array of dangerously-looking agricultural machinery.

The fine-looking building on your left dressed in limestone is the former court house.

From the old court house walk downhill for 100m and at the road junction take the road on your right which leads directly to the village, thus completing the fourth stage of the Kendal Limestone Way.

Ingleborough

Ingleborough (elevation 723m) is the second highest mountain in the Yorkshire Dales National Park, only exceeded by Whernside which is 14m higher.

The most noticeable feature of Ingleborough is its stepped sides indicating different types of rock. The summit plateau has a millstone grit cap which is impervious to rainwater, thus enabling the mountain to maintain its inimitable profile. At the base of the mountain lies a layer of carboniferous limestone and sandwiched between are alternative layers of limestone, sandstone and shales.

The stony summit plateau is surprisingly large covering an area of about 15 acres (6 hectares) and is slightly tilted. At one time the entire plateau was enclosed by a stone wall, a large part of which has been destroyed. Within the defensive wall are the remains of circular huts belonging to iron age people. However, some archaeologists have questioned this theory believing that the stone circles are in fact ring cairns used by bronze age people for ritual purposes. This would place the remains further back in time to about 1000BC.

The views from the summit rank amongst the very best in the Pennines with Whernside, Penyghent, Cam Fell, Simon Fell and Pendle all being prominent along with the Wenning Valley, the Lake District Fells, Twisleton Scars and the coastal incursions made by the shimmering waters of

Morecambe Bay. The non-natural feature of Ribblehead Viaduct viewed from the northern tip of the plateau is particularly impressive.

Windshelter, Ingleborough summit

Ingleborough from Crina Bottom

Clapham to Ingleton

Ingleton's most famous landmark, the railway viaduct, which once carried steam trains high above the River Greta

Ingleton

Geology

Ingleton lies at the foot of a glacial valley flanked by Ingleborough in the east and by the Whernside mastiff in the west. The centre of the village lies along the eastern escarpment of a steep-sided gorge scoured by the rivers Twiss and Doe. These two unusually named rivers, which merge at the viaduct to form the River Greta, create a natural phenomena of woodland glens and waterfalls that are considered the finest in England.

It is the Ingleton glens along with the spectacular caves and potholes in the surrounding hills for which Ingleton is renowned.

History

Ingleton's historical roots go back thousands of years. In the second millennium BC a Celtic tribe built and occupied a hill fort (the highest in the country) on the summit of Ingleborough. The remains of this Iron Age Settlement are still traceable today.

The Roman infantry marched through the village on its way between forts at Bainbridge and Lancaster. The Romans set up a signal station on Ingleborough using beacons of fire. In Celtic-Roman "Ingle" means fire. At the time of the Norman

Conquest Ingleton was known as "Inglstune", the fire town.

Industrial Heritage

The village lies on the edge of a massive bedrock of limestone which extends deep into the Yorkshire Dales. For hundreds of years limestone has been extensively quarried, an activity which continues to this day.

The buildings of Ingleton are predominantly built of grey limestone as is Ingleton's most famous landmark, the railway viaduct which carried the now abandoned Midland Railway line high above the River Greta.

The old court house, Ingleton

At one time Ingleton had a thriving coal mining industry employing up to 500 miners, but a major geological fault in the coal seam brought this activity to a premature end during the inter-war years.

The Industrial Revolution brought textile and tanning mills to the banks of the rivers Twiss and Doe and many of these long since abandoned mills have been converted into riverside apartments.

Parish Church

The parish Church of St Mary stands in a commanding position on a plateau high above the River Doe on a site formerly occupied by a Norman church. The tower is original built in the 13th-century but the nave is Victorian.

Pecca Falls, Ingleton Glens

No artist could fail to be inspired by Ingleton's maze of passageways lined with charming cottages

Ingleton has a mill town heritage

Ingleton to Kirkby Lonsdale

Distance: 11.4 miles (18.3 km)

Walking Time: 7 hours approximately

Terrain: Strenuous walking from Ingleton to Masongill mainly over rough fellsides and along partially enclosed lanes. The section between Kingsdale Beck and the Turbary Road is unremittingly steep. An alternative route from Kingsdale Beck to Masongill avoiding the steep valley wall climb to the Turbary Road is included in the narrative. From Masongill to Kirkby Lonsdale walking is easy to moderate as the route advances alongside watercourses, over grazing pastures and along ancient cart tracks.

Waymarking: Generally good throughout the route..

Map: 1:25 000 OS Explorer OL2 Yorkshire Dales Southern & Western areas.

A brief description of the route

The route leaves Ingleton, a village at the confluence of the rivers Twiss and Doe, for Scar End where it makes a left turn to briefly enter Kingsdale before climbing out of the valley on a steeply rising path that threads its way through huge blocks of limestone to join an ancient high-level track leading to the farming settlement of Masongill. Just beyond Masongill the route enters the attractive village of Ireby situated at the foot of Ireby Fell. The border with Lancashire is crossed as the route presses on towards the villages of Leck and Cowan Bridge. From Cowan Bridge, the route follows Leck Beck downstream before setting a course for Kirkby Lonsdale where the Kendal Limestone Way enters Cumbria via a remarkable three-arched, 15th-century bridge spanning the River Lune.

Accommodation: Kirkby Lonsdale offers a range of accommodation including inns with rooms, guest houses and B&Bs as well as a hotel overlooking the market-square. Within one mile of Kirkby Lonsdale are camping pitches. Lupton (half a mile off-route) has a refurbished inn with restaurant and rooms. Located one mile east of Kirkby Lonsdale on the A65 at Burrow with Burrow is Whoop Hall Inn, a hotel and country club. The Kendal Limestone Way passes within feet of this hotel. A little further away there is a boutique hotel located between Ireby and Cowan Bridge close to the A65.

Cafes, restaurants and tea-rooms: Kirkby Lonsdale has an excellent selection of eateries. Cowan Bridge has a tea-room which also sells sandwiches, cold drinks and general provisions.

Tourist Information Centre: Kirkby Lonsdale (limited services)

Post Offices: Kirkby Lonsdale

Village Shops: Cowan Bridge and Kirkby Lonsdale.

Ingleton to Kirkby Lonsdale

Chemists: Kirkby Lonsdale

Public Toilets: Kirkby Lonsdale and Devil's Bridge

Rail Services: The nearest mainline stations are at Oxenholme Kendal (11 miles 18km) and Lancaster (14 miles 23km). The nearest local station is at Wennington (5 miles 8km) on the Lancaster-Skipton-Leeds line.

Bus Services: Kirkby Lonsdale with connections to Lancaster, Kendal, Crooklands, Lupton, Cowan Bridge, Clapham and Austwick.

The Craven Connection operates a regular service between Kirkby Lonsdale and Skipton via Ingleton, Settle, Long Preston and Gargrave.

Alternative route to Kingsdale Beck

The alternative route to Kingsdale Beck is a classic being one-half of the famous "waterfalls walk". Every step through the charming glens is a delight. However, it should be noted that the "waterfalls walk" is over private ground and the estate owners charge for using their paths. Given that you are only treading on half the paths through the estate the charge is relatively steep and for a family fairly expensive.

The entrance to the "waterfalls walk" is signposted throughout the village. From the main street take the Thornton road and turn left after crossing the second bridge. The path to Kingsdale Beck follows the River Twiss upstream as it cascades down the valley. The path is clear throughout although extreme care must be taken in wet or icy conditions and children at all times closely supervised.

The two most impressive waterfalls en route to Kingsdale Beck are Pecca Falls and Thornton Force where the River Twiss leaps 14 metres over a bed of white limestone three hundred and fifty million years old.

From Thornton Force the path climbs open ground above the waterfall and after a short distance rejoins the river which is crossed via a footbridge. The path ascends the steep valley wall to meet a broad track known as Twisleton Lane. Turn left to rejoin the author's route.

Those who have eschewed the charms of the "waterfalls walk" should descend the steep road by the parish church, cross the first bridge and, before the second bridge, turn right onto Mill Lane where there once stood a large textile mill which came to an ignominious end in 1904 following a fire. After passing riverside apartments the lane narrows to a single track as it begins a remorselessly steep climb out of the village.

In late spring the banks bordering the lane are dotted with dog roses providing a pleasant distraction from the arduous climb. The lane (officially known as Oddie's Lane) serves isolated farmsteads located in the upper reaches of Chapel-le-Dale. It was originally a Roman road linking the Roman fort at Bainbridge in Wensleydale with the Lune Valley and Lancaster.

As height is gained ugly gashes left behind in the surrounding hillsides by the quarrying of limestone are all too evident. On the opposite side of the valley, under the shadow of a large limestone scar, is a modest single-storey building with the word *cave* painted on its roof. This is White Scar Cave, the largest show-cave in Britain.

A short distance beyond the driveway to Twisleton Manor, Oddies Lane inclines sharply to the right, and at the point where the lane starts to unwind pass through a metal gate on your left (not waymarked when last checked by the author but nevertheless a public right of way) that follows a tarmac track leading to a working

Thornton Force - a site of major geological interest

Alternative route to Masongill in poor visibility and/or avoiding the steep climb to the Turbary Road

On reaching the end of Twisleton Lane turn left but instead of taking the ladder stile on your right continue forward and after the brow of the hill take the first road on your right (Westgate Lane) which passes a radio station on your left. 400m beyond the radio station the road inclines to the left at which point go with the wide track on your right. This is Tow Scar Road which ultimately leads to the Turbary Road. After about a mile the rough track terminates alongside Masongill Fell Lane. Turn left and rejoin the author's route to Masongill.

Kingsdale, settled by the Vikings

farm grandly ascribed as *Twisleton Hall* by the Ordnance Survey, no doubt reflecting its status in former times.

Pass through the farmyard and on meeting the "waterfalls walk" track turn left passing two dwellings on your left. About 200m from the last building you will notice a bridleway path zigzaging up the shoulder of the hill. This is not our route but in former times the path was an ancient packhorse route, known as *Craven Old Way*.

Craven Old Way

Craven Old Way was a high-level track between Ingleton and Dentdale used by foot travellers and packhorse "trains". From medieval times to the coming of the turnpikes, a period of some five hundred years, packhorses (20 to 40 ponies made up a typical "train") were used for transporting coal, iron ore, lead, wool and general merchandise between the Dales. The old packhorse routes can usually be identified by a zigzag path wending its way up the fellside before levelling out into a high-level causeway.

Continue forward passing in high summer an ice-cream vendor whose van is strategically placed to capture the trade from the waterfall walkers struggling up the steep incline above Thornton Force.

Shortly you arrive at a footbridge crossing Kingsdale Beck (the River Twiss in all but name). The views from the bridge towards the head of Kingsdale are sublime. The flat-bottomed valley was settled by the Vikings over a thousand years ago. Great walls of

rock-shattered limestone encircle the valley.

Ahead lies a narrow ribbon of tarmac linking Kingsdale with Dent. On reaching the road turn left and after 50m take the ladder stile on your right. A quick glance at the OS map will reveal a "straight-as-an-arrow" path ascending the valley wall. If only this were so In reality the path will test your navigational skills not to mention your stamina as it meanders around the huge shattered limestone rocks littering the exceptionally steep fellside.

Initially aim for a stone wall running horizontally below the steepest section of the valley wall before homing in on a substantial ladder stile set amongst enormous limestone boulders. On descending the dizzy heights of the stile you will notice a wall on your right running up the fellside. The path leading to the Turbary Road runs to the left of this wall but it does not hug the wall.

On reaching the Turbary Road - in reality a cart-track adopting a natural shelf between the grassy slopes of Gragareth and the fractured limestone of Keld Head Scar - turn left and walk forward.

The views eastwards are dominated by the western flank of Ingleborough and stand comparison in scenic terms with the best views of the mountain seen on the walk.

At the junction of Tow Scar Road (signed *Westgate Lane*) the rough cart-track matures into a surfaced lane. Stay with the downward sloping lane until you reach the outskirts of Masongill, one mile away. The route bypasses the tiny hamlet of

Masongill where Arthur Conan Doyle, the creator of the world's most famous detective, Sherlock Holmes, was a frequent visitor. To visit the handsome tree-lined settlement head towards the old telephone kiosk which can be seen from Fell Lane.

Returning to Fell Lane and within sight of the telephone kiosk you should notice a metal gate against which stands a less than obvious waymarker. This is our route. Go with the wall on your left. After 250m or so the path forks. Take the left branch which bears round to a lovely enclosed green lane; this terminates all too soon above a gorse-lined gill through which Ireby Beck flows.

At this delightful spot we take our leave of the white rose county as we slip across the unmarked border into Lancashire. Pass through two metal gates located above the banks of the gill before crossing a large pasture above Over Hall. The path is waymarked and runs to the left of a belt of trees above the hall. The path terminates in front of a kissing gate accessing the driveway leading to the hall. Walk away from the hall towards Ireby (the name means "the town of the Irish Vikings"). Clusters of attractive cottages, some dating back to the 17th-century, straddle its eponymous beck. Two bridges - one an ancient clapper bridge and the other a small road bridge opposite

Turbary Road

"Turbary" is an ancient common law right possessed by tenants of the manor to cut turf or peat for fuel upon another man's land. In former times the peat was dug in early summer from pastures above Yordas Cave and, after drying, transported via cart along the track leading to Thornton.

The historic rights of turbary largely died out during the 19th-century when coal for fuel became more widely available.

For those whose interests extend to the subterranean world of caverns, passages and underground streams accessed by frighteningly deep holes in the ground will find a walk along the Turbary Road towards the head of Kingsdale immensely satisfying. Lining both sides of the road are numerous caves and potholes, the most famous being Rowten Pot, a highly dangerous chasm which extends hundreds of feet into the deep limestone recesses of Kingsdale.

At the northern end of the road is Yordas Cave set amongst trees on private land. In Victorian times it was a show-cave and according to legend the lair of a Norse giant, Yordas, whose extra-curricular activities are the stuff of nightmares. It is thought that Emily Bronte visited the cave and provided a fictionalised account in Wuthering Heights.

Swinsto Hole, Simpson's Pot and Jingling Pot all lie close to the road and all potentially dangerous to non-cavers and potholers.

Bridge House - provide a dry crossing of the beck.

Walk down the main street and at the first junction go with the road on your right. At the second junction bear right and continue along the narrow road for 500m. When you reach Todgill Farm, sited on a sharp bend on your left, walk no further along the road. On your right an unsurfaced lane peels away from the road. This is our route for the next mile. After half a mile the delightful lane passes to the right of Leck Hall built in 1801 and today the family seat of Lord Shuttleworth. The hall is not open to the public.

In springtime the plantations on your right play host to great swathes of bluebells which carpet the woodland floor.

At the end of the lane turn left (if you turn right either by mistake or intentionally the narrow road leads to Leck Fell). After 700m you arrive at a sharp bend. On your left just beyond the bend stands Bank House Farm. On the opposite side of the road to the farm, close to the bend, you should notice a waymark post standing alongside a metal gate. The post denotes a path which falls away towards a broad pasture above Leck Beck. This is our route.

On gaining the beck follow it for a short distance downstream and then take the ladder stile accessing a broad track which matures into Low Lane. Press on forward passing a cluster of old buildings, one of which is a former mill. You have reached the northern outpost of Leck. The name is derived from the Norse *Locke* meaning brook.

Where the lane forks take the right branch

Leck Fell

Leck Fell occupies a narrow corridor of land between Cumbria and the Yorkshire Dales National Park (as presently constituted although at the time of writing the Department for Environment, Food and Rural Affairs has approved plans to extend the Yorkshire Dales National Park westwards to include areas of north Lancashire, including Leck Fell, and east Cumbria).

Leck Fell at 628m is the highest point in Lancashire.

It is often thought that the Yorkshire Limestone Dales have the most extensive natural underground passages in Britain. Few realise that in this remote and barren corner of Lancashire a labyrinth of potholes provide access to the Lancaster pot system, the longest underground cave system in Britain.

which leads to a row of uniform-style houses on your left. 100m beyond these dwellings on the same side of the road is a farm. Opposite the farm on your right is a waymarker attached to a lamppost. A gap stile leads into a field. Make your way across the field and rejoin the path that follows Leck Beck downstream.

If you are lucky you might just catch sight of a salmon migrating upstream to spawn in the higher reaches of the beck which rises out of Leck Fell.

The well-trodden path passes below a disused railway viaduct. 100m beyond the viaduct the path terminates in front of a small gate and stile admitting to Cowan Bridge which carries the busy A65 across Leck Beck.

The village of Cowan Bridge, which straddles the A65, has a popular shop and tea-room selling hot and cold drinks, ice-cream, sandwiches etc. To reach the shop (which is slightly off-route) turn left and walk forward for 200m.

To regain the route cross the busy A65 with great care as the view along the carriageway on your right is restricted by a bend. Cross the old bridge, which is built a few feet downstream of the new bridge carrying the A65 traffic, and follow the waymarked path down to the riverbank. The old building on your right has an interesting place in English literature.

Jane Eyre

In Charlotte Bronte's great social novel, the young Jane Eyre is sent to Lowood, a school for poor and orphaned girls. The conditions at the school were absolutely dreadful - bitterly cold rooms, poor food and inadequate clothing to cope with the harsh winters of northern England. Typhus is endemic. In one of the most moving passages in English literature Jane's fellow pupil and close friend, Helen Burns, dies of tuberculosis in her arms.

A plaque on the gable end of the former school commemorates the Bronte connection. In 1824 the building was opened as a school for the daughters of clergymen. The Rev. Patrick Bronte sent four of his five daughters to the school - Maria, Elizabeth, Emily and Charlotte. All four children had a miserable time and pleaded with their father "to get us out of this place". After one year at the school illness forced their return to Howarth.

Elizabeth and Maria died of tuberculosis in 1825.

In 1833 the school closed and moved to its present site at Casterton above Kirkby Lonsdale.

Jane Eyre was first published in 1847 and five chapters of the book are devoted to Jane's time at Lowood.

Follow the beckside path (which eventually matures into a tarmac farm access track) for some 600m at which point you will notice a cluster of buildings on the far side of Leck Beck accessed via a metal bridge.

The tiny hamlet is known as Overtown and lies on the course of a former Roman road from Manchester to Carlisle. Less than a mile away the Romans built a fort at Burrow-in-Lonsdale where one thousand troops were billeted. The site has been excavated but little remains above ground of the Roman occupation. It is likely that the fort at Burrow and Overtown were connected by a spur road.

From the bridge walk forward for 50m and take the stile next to a wooden gate on your right just in front of a cattle grid. The stile admits to a large pasture. Ignore the waymarked path which runs away to your left. Our path is straight ahead, initially maintaining contact with a wire fence on your right and then a hedge.

Continue on the same course crossing a stile leading to a small stream. Cross the stream via a footbridge and maintaining the same course aim for the south-east corner of a plantation over to your left. The path now runs north alongside a hedge on your left and terminates on meeting a small stream running below the southern boundary of a caravan park. Enter and cross the park on the public path which leads to an exit stile on the park's western boundary. Immediately beyond the stile a leftward slanting path runs across two pastures towards Whoop Hall Inn. Two gates lead into the surprisingly large grounds of the hotel. The public path runs along the top of an embankment before joining the hotel access road. Follow the road round to the A65.

At the end of the hotel driveway walk a few steps rightwards and locate a stile admitting to a large pasture on the far side of the road. With extreme care cross the busy A65 and enter the pasture via the stile. The path runs below a hedge on your left at the end of which there are a plethora of metal gates leading into the next pasture.

Upon reaching the third pasture in the series the path switches from the left-hand side of the hedge to the right.

The fourth field crossed by the path is invariably put to arable use and the driver of the tractor has been known without any consideration for walkers to plough right up to the hawthorn hedge on your right, thus making walking along the public path a struggle.

At the end of this field cross the farm access track and proceed through a metal gate accessing a green lane. Walk to the end of the lane, turn left and walk down the quiet country road towards the settlement of Chapel House where the road bends sharply to the right. Stay with the road and at the minor junction proceed forward passing on your right the entrance to a static caravan park. The tarmac track winds down an embankment at the foot of which stands a large boulder. At this point bear right and walk towards the Hawes road passing a roadside car park on the way.

Cross the Hawes road and head for a cabin located on the access road to Devil's Bridge. The cabin does a rip-roaring trade in bacon butties and hot and cold drinks..

If you happen to arrive at this local beauty spot on a Sunday or a public holiday then you may feel you have inadvertently gate-crashed a Harley Davidson convention such is the popularity of the bridge amongst the motor cycling fraternity.

Cross the ancient three-arched bridge spanning the River Lune. The bridge is a scheduled ancient monument and marks the boundary between Lancashire and Cumbria.

NB There are shorter ways into Kirkby Lonsdale but the one described below is by far the most picturesque and interesting.

Immediately beyond the bridge take the first path on your right which follows the Lune upstream for three quarters of a mile passing on your left old mills which once formed the industrial heartland of the town but now converted into character dwellings. When you reach the *Radical Steps* (signed) built around 1830 by a local doctor with so-called liberal views take a deep breath for before you are a flight of eight-five steps.

On reaching the top step turn right and 70m along the embankment you will come to a plaque marking a viewpoint known as *Ruskin's View*.

On a clear day the view across the riverside meadows and woods towards Brownthwaite and the Middleton Fells is indeed lovely but it highly questionable whether it justifies the sobriquet "one of the loveliest scenes in England".

Map 17

Ruskin's View

Having established that Ruskin was not adverse to using the occasional hyperbolic phrase in support of his friend Turner, retrace your steps towards the *Radical Steps* and enter the grounds of the parish church of St Mary.

The church is an absolute gem standing in the midst of centuries old weathered grave stones surrounded by warm limestone cottages, the whole set against a backdrop of rolling green hills.

In this loveliest of churchyards (to paraphrase Ruskin) we complete the fifth stage of our walk to Kendal.

In 1818 the artist, J.M.W. Turner, painted the prospect of the Lune Valley and surrounding hills from the churchyard. On seeing the painting, Turner's friend, the art critic and philosopher, John Ruskin, declared: "Here are moorland, sweet river and English forest at their best" and the view "one of the loveliest scenes in England and therefore in the world".

Kirkby Lonsdale

The devil may have had a hand in building its famous bridge but surely it was the gods who looked favourably upon the development of Kirkby Lonsdale into a prosperous country town that it is today. It is

The River Lune below Kirkby Lonsdale

almost too perfect to be true. It lies mid-way between the Lakes and the Yorkshire Dales, just off the A65 and within a few miles of the M6 motorway. The central area of the town lies on a high bank overlooking a bend in the River Lune.

The town is surrounded by hills which provide a degree of protection from the winter storms which blow across the Pennines and Cumbrian Fells. Spring comes early to this part of the Lune Valley as Morecambe Bay with the warm currents of the gulf stream lapping its shores is not far away.

History

At the time of the Domesday Survey the town was known as "Cherchebi", that is "Church town in Lonsdale".

Resplendent iron gates leading to the parish church

Main street, Kirkby Lonsdale

Ingleton to Kirkby Lonsdale

The Lune Valley has the second highest concentration of Norman castle sites in England. Kirkby Lonsdale occupies what was once an important strategic position above the Lune. The Normans built a motte-and-bailey on a hill close to the parish church. The site later became known as "Cockpit Hill" for obvious reasons.

The oldest building in Kirkby Lonsdale is the church dedicated to Saint Mary the virgin and which stands near the site of an earlier Saxon church. The present church dates back to the 12th-century although much restoration work was carried out in Victorian times and more recently. However, the interior of the church still retains many original features dating back to the Norman period.

In 1227 the king granted a licence for the town to hold a weekly market which is now held every Thursday in the "new" market square built in 1832 to meet the increase in trade brought about by the town's increasing prosperity.

Devil's Bridge, as it is known locally, was built in the 15th-century (circa) and replaced an earlier structure dating back to the 13th-century or possibly even earlier. It was closed to traffic in 1932 when Stanley Bridge was built a short distance downstream to carry the town's new bypass. Prior to the bypass all traffic from Yorkshire and Lancashire to the Lake District passed through the town centre.

The streets in the old part of the town have some interesting names: Salt Pie Lane, and Jingling Lane to name but two.

Devil's Bridge spanning the River Lune

79

St Mary's Church, Kirkby Lonsdale

Kirkby Lonsdale to Levens Bridge

Distance: 11.4 miles (18.3km)

Walking Time: 6 hours approximately

Terrain: Easy walking mainly across grazing pastures from Kirkby Lonsdale to Hutton Roof. Moderate walking across Hutton Roof Crags and Farleton Fell. Easy walking from Farleton village to Levens Bridge along canal tow paths (where tree roots are a potential hazard) and farm tracks.

Waymarking: Generally poor between Kirkby Lonsdale and Farleton village. Excellent from Farleton village to Levens Bridge.

Maps: (1) 1:25 000 OS Explorer OL2 Yorkshire Dales Southern & Western areas, and (2) 1:25 000 OS Explorer OL7 The English Lakes South-eastern area.

A brief description of the route

From Kirkby Lonsdale the route passes though the settlements of Low and High Biggins before adopting the Limestone Link footpath to Hutton Roof, a village lying under the eastern lee of Hutton Roof Crags. On a rising path running between outcrops of limestone the route climbs the fellside before veering away to join a path linking Hutton Roof Crags with neighbouring Farleton Fell. The route contours along the north-eastern flank of Farleton Fell above the tiny hamlet of Newbiggin.

On reaching Farleton, a village five miles from the shores of Morecambe Bay, the route joins the towpath of the Lancaster Canal which it follows northwards passing underneath the M6 motorway and through the village of Crooklands to Stainton Bridge, the terminus of the canal. Just beyond Stainton Bridge the route passes below the busy A590 and the main west coast railway line between London, the Midlands and Scotland as it progresses to Hincaster and its eponymous tunnel. From the entrance of the tunnel the route takes an overland course to Hincaster Hall before setting a course for Levens Bridge where in front of Levens Hall, the penultimate section of the Kendal Limestone Way terminates.

Accommodation: Lupton (half a mile off-route on the A65) offers the Plough, a refurbished inn with restaurant and rooms. Crooklands has a roadside hotel. Sizergh offers Heaves, a long-established country house hotel just off the A590 and with the advantage of being en route. The Villa, a new fully restored country house hotel, has opened at Levens, close to the A590. Gilpin Bridge (one and a half miles off-route and close to the A590) has an inn with rooms.

Cafes and tea-rooms: A65/Lancaster Canal popular hideaway café and tea-room. Levens Hall Buttery (seasonal) serves lunches and light refreshments.

Public Houses: Lupton (half a mile off-route), Crooklands, Sizerth, Levens village (slightly off-route) and Gilpin Bridge (one and half miles off-route).

81

Kirkby Lonsdale to Levens Bridge

Rail Services: The nearest mainline stations are at Oxenholme Kendal 11 miles (18km) away, and Lancaster 14 miles (23km).away. The nearest local stations are at Arnside (off-route) and Grange-over-Sands (off-route) both on the Lancaster-Barrow-in-Furness line.

Bus Services: Lupton (half a mile off-route) and Crooklands with services to Kendal and Kirkby Lonsdale.

From Levens Bridge there are regular bus services to Carnforth, Lancaster, Kendal, Windermere, Ambleside, Grasmere and Keswick.

From the market square walk up Mitchelgate passing on your left the access road to Booths, a supermarket group with a strong presence in north-west England. At the T junction bear left and continue forward along Biggins Road passing through the grounds of Queen Elizabeth School.

Cross the A65 with care and walk up Biggins Road passing on your left a telephone kiosk. About 70m beyond the kiosk on your right you will find a fingerpost inscribed *High Biggins*. A metal kissing gate admits to a field with a path crossing its top edge. A second kissing gate accesses a wood through which a well-trodden path weaves through the trees. Exit the wood via a third kissing gate and walk forward passing in front of Biggins Hall.

Continue along the lane passing on your right a Day Nursery and Community Centre. At the junction ignore the road on your left. Pass in front of Biggins Lodge Farm and walk up hill for 300m pausing when you reach a lane end on your left.

At the end of the lane below an electricity pylon you will notice a gap stile which in high summer is partially concealed by nettles.

next objective, the route adopts a short section of the *Limestone Link*, a long-distance path between Kirkby Lonsdale and the Kent estuary town of Arnside. For a local authority sponsored route the waymarking is extremely poor and for the next two miles it is not difficult to get lost as the author did on researching this section of the route.

Pass through the gap stile and walk diagonally across the foot of the pasture. Do not aim too high or you will miss the stile in

the hedge admitting to a narrow path. A second stile provides access to a large grazing pasture. Go round the sheep pens and proceed up the pasture on a left-leaning course with a hedge on your right but keeping well to the right of a broken line of trees over to your left.

Locate and take the stile into the second pasture and maintain the same direction of travel. On entering the third pasture in the series pause after walking 100m. On the western boundary of the pasture (that is in the direction of travel) there is a metal gate which at this distance appears to be below a pylon. Aim for the gate guided by a low ridge of limestone rocks. Proceed through the gate where you are immediately confronted by two waymarked paths. Ignore the path crossing the pasture on a westerly course in favour of the slanting path that runs downhill towards a derelict barn at the foot of the pasture.

Enter the next pasture and simply follow uphill the power lines eventually passing a little to the right of Longfield Tarn.

From the tarn the path, still in the shadow of the power lines, takes a downhill course and comes to rest at the head of a lane bordered on one side by a stream and on the other by a wall.

On reaching the road turn left and walk forward to a T junction. Turn left again, cross the road and (unless visiting Hutton Roof, a linear village with its roots in farming and offering little in the way of historical or archaeological interest) go with the track which runs below the gable end of Glebe Cottage (signed *Hutton Roof Crags*). After 100m the broad track narrows to a single file path. Proceed through a wooden gate and continue up the hill maintaining contact with the wall on your right.

After a short distance the narrow path matures into a broad green sward which forks after 250m. Take the left branch which pursues a higher course up the hill.

After a short distance the path forks yet again. This time overlook the left branch as this leads to a wall of limestone where novices are taught the rudimentary techniques of rock climbing by trained instructors.

Keep true to the outer path which levels out as it contours around the northern slopes of the fell in the form of a balcony before entering an ancient wood containing fine examples of trees not normally found in British woodland.

Ten minutes or so later the path emerges from the shade to regain the open balcony with higher ground over to your left and three farmsteads nestling at the foot of the fell below. Ahead lies Farleton Fell, our next objective.

Hutton Roof Crags and Farleton Fell are divided by geography and an unclassified road that runs between the two fells. Our path joins the road which is where we take our leave of the *Limestone Link* path. Turn right and walk a few paces to the cross-roads and then take the farm access road on your left; this leads down to Whin Yeats Farm and a Caravan Club licensed site.

The concrete road down to the farm offers fine views to the Middleton Fells above Kirkby Lonsdale and the blue-tinted

Morecambe Bay Limestone Pavements

The upland Morecambe Bay area is blessed with a rich variety of limestone scenery and Hutton Roof Crags and Newbiggin Crags on Farleton Fell are noted for their limestone pavements.

The limestone pavement flora is diverse and is protected by being included in a Special Area of Conservation under regulation enacted by Parliament.

The two fells have a rich diversity of trees including yew, juniper, buckthorn, hazel, small leaved lime and ash.

Howgills. The green eminence rising above Lupton Beck and bedecked with twin telecon masts is Scout Hill.

Pass through two metal gates leading to the farm. About 100m after the second gate walk towards the farmhouse with its interesting bovine weathervane and divert to a wall on your left with a waymarker. The wall is directly opposite the farmhouse. A large metal gate leads to the open fell above the farm. Follow the track to a wooden gate beyond which a broad green track unfolds.

Proceed forward disregarding all subsidiary tracks and paths leading off to the left.

When you reach a waymark post go with the path on your right. As you advance along the north-eastern flank of the fell the higher ground on your left is occupied by Newbiggin Crags. Over to your right are the roof tops of Newbiggin, a tiny settlement lying under the northern lee of the fell.

The bridleway eventually terminates in front of a metal gate admitting to a lane. Turn right and follow the short lane down to a white bungalow on your right. A second small gate accesses a surfaced lane with the curious name of *Puddlemire*. Turn left and walk down Puddlemire, a lane gated at the beginning and end of the open fell section. Scenic interest is provided by the distant Lakeland hills, the Howgill fells and closer to home the Lupton Valley with Scout Hill rising above its beck.

On reaching the second gate pause for a moment. Our route is straight ahead but the road on your right serves as a short-cut to Lupton, a hamlet straddling the A65 where the Plough Inn provides food and accommodation. There is also a bus stop outside the Plough Inn with regular services to Kendal and Kirkby Lonsdale.

From the gate walk forward for half a mile and on reaching the road junction bear left. Continue until you reach a farm on your left that lies on the northern perimeter of Farleton, a hamlet nestling at the foot of Farleton Fell. Opposite the farm a narrow lane leads to a bridge crossing the Lancaster Canal.

Cross the bridge and on joining the canal towpath turn left. The canal will be our watery companion for the next six miles as we explore its northern reaches.

The walk along the towpath is undemanding and navigation straightforward. The canal marks the boundary between the flat coastal plain on your left where the land is put to arable use and the undulating grazing land on your right where livestock farming prevails.

The Lancaster Canal

In 1792 worked started on a canal system that would provide passage between Preston and Kendal via Lancaster. From the start the work was beset by engineering difficulties and cost overruns. It was not until 1819 that the full length of the canal was open to travellers and freight.

The canal became known as "the black and white" as it would bring coal from Lancashire to Kendal and limestone from Westmorland to Lancashire.

The coming of the railways rapidly put an end to passenger traffic and the last commercial freight was carried in 1947.

The final hammer blow was struck with the building of the M6 motorway in the 1960s. This cut off the northern reaches beyond Lancaster.

Made redundant by the railway, dismembered by the motorway, the ultimate ignominy came to the luckless canal with the draining of the section between Kendal and Stainton. Here forlorn bridges, like ghosts in the night, mysteriously cross dry land.

A trust has been formed with the objective of re-opening the northern reaches of the canal but the cost would be enormous and it is doubtful whether its ambitious, though entirely laudable, aims will ever be fully realized.

Ahead lies the A65. On the opposite bank stand a cluster of buildings including a popular café with a terrace overlooking the canal. To visit the café leave the towpath at bridge 162. The canal slips silently under the A65 unnoticed by motorists speeding

Looking back towards Farleton Fell

between the Lake District and the Yorkshire Dales. The complex of buildings on your left includes a farmers' cattle market.

The canal is now heading towards Crooklands where the M6 motorway forms a barrier which temporarily suspends the towpath. Pass under the motorway bridge. A small gate on your left admits to a path that crosses the head of the canal from where the towpath can be rejoined.

Continue along the towpath passing the Waterwitch, a traditionally designed narrowboat which cruises the northern reaches of the canal above Crooklands.

Crooklands hosts the Westmorland

Annual Show in September. As you approach bridge 168 the showground is sited on your left-hand side.

As we advance into the upper reaches, the canal takes on the appearance of a tranquil river.

Storks are a common sight amongst the reed beds. A family of swans duck and dive for food in water warmed by the summer sun. Electric-blue dragon flies flit from bank to bank. A shoal of minnows swimming in unison nervously dart one way and cartwheel the other as they explore the shallows.

Bridge 172 at Stainton marks the end of the .

Lancaster Canal but not the towpath which continues for another 700m above a waterless but reed strewn canal bed except where natural pools fed by rainwater have settled.

At the end of the towpath a stile to the left of a metal gate admits to a surfaced road. Turn left and proceed under the bridge carrying the A591 Kendal bypass. Just beyond the bridge on your right are two fingerposts - one inscribed *Kendal* and the other *Hincaster*. The latter is our route.

Pass through the gate and follow the path, which turns away from the noisy dual carriageway, towards Hincaster tunnel. A side path leads down to the old canal tunnel which is full of water.

Having satisfied yourself that there is, after

Ducking and diving

all, light at the end of the tunnel take the stone steps leading back to the main path. The well-worn path passes through two small tunnels, the second of which goes under the main west coast line where Pendolino tilting trains hurtle along at great speed just a few feet above your head!

Exploring the northern reaches

87

The partly enclosed path climbs Hincaster Hill before descending towards a cluster of dwellings forming the northern outpost of Hincaster.

On reaching a small bridge cast your eyes up and in the middle distance you should spot, depending on visibility, our next objective, Hincaster Hall.

As you approach the road a sign on your left directs to *Levens Hall via public footpath*. This is our route. Ignore the path to Kendal.

Hincaster, the village, lies to the left of the junction and although pleasant enough there is little of interest to merit a detour.

Cross the road and follow the lane uphill passing a white-washed cottage on your right.

Opposite the entrance to the hall, a Grade II listed building built late 16th-century, a fingerpost directs to a public footpath that winds around the western perimeter of the hall before seeking out higher ground above it. Follow this path which shortly matures into a farm access track.

The views retrospectively are pleasant enough but they are over-shadowed by the views straight ahead, notably the long limestone escarpment of Whitbarrow and its Lakeland companions.

The right of way passes to the left of substantial farm outbuildings before turning to pass in front of a three-storey farmhouse with heavy round chimneys redolent of the vernacular architecture common in this part of the old county of Westmorland.

Hincaster Tunnel

The Hincaster Tunnel, opened in June 1819, is a scheduled ancient monument. It is 346m long lined with approximately four million bricks made locally at Heversham. The portals at both ends of the tunnel are limestone faced.

There is no towpath running through the tunnel and the bargees were pulled through by means of a chain fixed to the tunnel walling.

The towing horses were led over Hincaster Hill to rejoin their barge on the other side.

The west coast main line runs above the tunnel.

The concrete track now sets a bee-line for Levens Hall with its deer park on the far side of the estate wall over to your right.

At the end of the concrete track a cattle grid is crossed and a fragmented tarmac roadway leads to the A6 with Levens Hall and its world famous topiary garden opposite.

On reaching the main road turn right and cross Levens Bridge, thus completing the sixth and penultimate stage of our walk to Kendal.

Levens Bridge to Kendal

Distance: 9.2 miles (14.8km)

Walking Time: 5 hours approximately.

Terrain: Easy to moderate walking throughout the route.

Waymarking: Excellent although Serpentine Wood at Kendal can be confusing for first-time visitors.

A brief description of the route

The final leg of the walk to Kendal starts from Levens Bridge where the route crosses the River Kent which it initially follows upstream through the deer park of Levens Hall. Beyond the deer park the route crosses the A590 en route to Sizergh Castle, owned by the National Trust. The Kendal Limestone Way passes in front of the castle as it advances towards Helsington Church, built on the edge of an escarpment overlooking the Lyth Valley and the Coniston Fells.

From Helsington Church the route crosses the Brigsteer Road and on a rising path ascends Underbarrow Scar (locally known as Scout Scar, a mile long limestone ridge). After crossing Underbarrow Road the route presses on towards a cairn located at the northern tip of Cunswick Scar. From the cairn the route falls away towards the Kendal bypass which is crossed via a footbridge.

On a gently rising path the route strikes a course for the northern perimeter of Kendal Golf Course and Serpentine Wood. After emerging from the wood the route makes a steep descent into Kendal close to Castle Howe (the site of a 12th-century motte-and-bailey) and the old Town Hall.

The Kendal Limestone Way terminates in the grounds of the medieval parish church built on a site above the River Kent in the ancient township of Kirkland.

Accommodation: Kendal offers a good selection of hotels to suit most budgets including inns with rooms, guest houses and b&bs. Centrally situated in Highgate, next to the Brewery Arts Centre, is an independently run hostel with 14 rooms. Levens has a recently opened luxury hotel named The Villa, just off the A590. Sizerth offers Heaves, a long-established country house hotel. Gilpin Bridge near Levens on the A5074 (off-route) has an inn with rooms. Windermere and Bowness (both less than 10 miles (16km) from Kendal) offer a wide range of accommodation as does Ambleside (13 miles (21km) from Kendal).

Cafes, restaurants and tea-rooms.   Kendal has an excellent selection of eateries. Levens Hall and Sizerth Castle (both seasonal) serve light meals and refreshments.

Levens Bridge to Kendal

Public Houses: Kendal, Sizerth, Levens village (slightly off route) and Brigsteer (slightly off route).

Tourist Information Centre: Kendal

Post Offices: Kendal

Village Shop: Levens village (slightly off-route)

Chemists: Kendal

Public Toilets: Kendal

Rail Services: Kendal station with local services to Windermere and Oxenholme. Oxenholme is 2.3miles (3.6km) from Kendal on the west coast mainline with frequent services to (1) London, the Midlands and Scotland and (2) Carlisle, Lancaster, Preston, Wigan, Warrington (connections to Liverpool, Manchester, Leeds, York, Middlesborough and Newcastle), Crewe and Birmingham.

Bus Services: Bus stops at Levens Bridge with connections to Lancaster, Carnforth and Kendal.

National Express operate services to and from Kendal.

Kendal Bus Station with services to Kirkby Lonsdale, Newby Bridge, Ulverston, Barrow-in-Furness, Windermere, Ambleside, Grasmere, Keswick, Penrith and other local destinations.

Levens Bridge

Having crossed Levens Bridge pass through the metal gate on your right signed *Park Head* and follow the well-walked path which initially heads towards the River Kent before swinging uphill through the landscaped deer park. The park is beautiful at any time of year but in late autumn when the beech and oak trees above the looping Kent put on a peerless display of autumnal colour it is absolutely stunning.

The public path through the park is waymarked. As you advance keep an eye open for the herd of black farrow deer. They are remarkably shy creatures.

Monsieur Beaumont

The mastermind behind the park and topiary gardens next to Levens Hall was a Frenchman, Monsieur Beaumont, who worked at Louis XIV's gardens at Versailles. Between 1694 and 1710 Beaumont redesigned the medieval deer park into the landscaped parkland we see today.

The path eventually terminates against a stepped stile built into the estate wall. The stile admits to a narrow pasture. Turn right and walk up the long pasture which, after rain, can be heavy going through the

91

Levens Bridge to Kendal

Levens Hall and Gardens

The Lake District has a world-class attraction in the topiary gardens at Levens Hall which were created in 1694. There are over one hundred individual topiary pieces made of evergreen yew and various forms of box clipped to unusual geometric designs. The topiary gardens are the oldest and most extensive of their kind in the world.

The hall is mainly Elizabethan with some 19th-century additions although at its core is a defensive pele tower built in 1300 (circa) to withstand Scottish raids.

Levens Hall, gardens and deer park are in private ownership. The hall is a private home but it is open along with the gardens between spring and autumn by permission of the Bagot family.

Levens Hall

Levens deer park in late autumn

upturned mud. Cross a second stepped stile and continue forward aiming for a huddle of buildings (Park Head) beyond the far right corner of the pasture. A wooden gate leads to a farm lane. Turn left and walk down the lane to the busy A590.

With extreme care cross the dual-carriageway and walk a few metres down to the T junction signed *Sizergh*. This is our route. Walk up the lane passing on your left the entrance to Heaves Hotel. Bear right at the first and second junctions and continue forward for about 450m.

On reaching a row of secluded limestone cottages set back from the road on your left take the broad track which runs in front and to the side of the cottages. The track leads to a waymarked path which, after a short distance, draws up alongside a kissing gate. Beyond the gate the path crosses a stream via a low-level footbridge. Proceed up the pasture with the plantation on your right. On reaching the top of the pasture turn right and after two stiles follow the path which maintains close contact with a long stone wall on your right. The path terminates against a gate leading to the National Trust car park for Sizergh Castle.

Walk down the car park passing in front of the restaurant and popular café.

At the far end of the car park look for a signpost inscribed *Helsington Church*. This is our route. Exit the car park via a wooden gate, cross the track and take the gate opposite that leads into a pasture crossed by a National Trust path. Cross the second pasture on a gently rising track leading to a large barn. Bear left at the barn, pass through a large wooden gate and press on to a second smaller gate accessing a charming

Westmorland

The old county of Westmorland was swept away by Parliament in 1974 following a massive local authority reorganisation.

Cumbria was created in the same year by merging the counties of (1) Westmorland (2) Cumberland (3) the north-western tip of Lancashire known as "Lancashire North of the Sands" and (4) the western extremities of the West Riding of Yorkshire.

In the hearts and minds of its people Westmorland lives on and the name is still common currency. Examples include the Westmorland County Show, the Westmorland Gazette and the Westmorland General Hospital.

wood whose banks in late spring are enlivened by colourful displays of bluebells and allium ursinum (wild garlic).

Exit the wood via a wooden gate, turn left and follow the broad track to Holeslack Farm which has undergone conversion to National Trust holiday cottages. A wooden gate admits to a concrete roadway that morphs into a crushed limestone track which in turn leads to a National Trust gate. Pass through the gate and continue forward disregarding the waymarked track peeling away on your left-hand side. Open fields unfold on your right. The woodland on your left shortly gives way to open pastures above the Lyth Valley. Ahead is Helsington Church (its Sunday name is St John's Church in the parish of Helsington).

The church serves the village of Brigsteer

Levens Bridge to Kendal

Sizergh Castle

According to Nikolaus Pevsner Sizergh *"is the most impressive house in Westmorland of the type consisting of pele tower, hall range, and later enlargements".*

The pele tower was built in or about 1340 to withstand Scottish raids. The tower is still intact and one of the largest and best preserved of its kind in England.

The great hall was built alongside the pele tower in 1450 with additions and alterations being added during the reign of Elizabeth I. *"No other house in England"* added Pevsner *"has such a wealth of Early Elizabethan woodwork of high quality."*

Sizergh Castle has been the home of the Strickland family for over seven hundred years. The early Stricklands were renowned fighters but like the Cliffords at Skipton Castle, invariably ending up on the losing side. A Strickland fought at Agincourt but the family backed the losing side in the War of the Roses and supported the royalist cause in the Civil War for which they paid a high price.

The castle and grounds are owned by the National Trust and are open to the public at published times.

Sizerth Castle

which lies at the foot of the escarpment. Rustic in character the church was built in 1726 although with substantial restoration in the 19th-century.

The church provides an ideal spot to get one's bearings and to test one's knowledge of the main Lakeland fells with the aid of the three-part toposcope overlooking the Lyth Valley, a valley, incidentally, famed for its damsons (a type of plum) which have been grown here since the 1700s.

The river meandering along the floor of the valley is the Gilpin whose waters drain into the River Kent. The prominent ridge across the valley is Whitbarrow but its dramatic "sea-like" cliffs are reserved for the delectation of motorists travelling on the A590 towards Newby Bridge.

A dappled glade
(Holeslack)

Working the fields above Sizergh Castle

Looking westwards over and beyond the Lyth Valley the Coniston Fells provide the main focus of interest. Scar Fell Pike, Bowfell, Great Gable and most of the other iconic Lakeland summits are visible on a clear day.

From the church continue along the road, now surfaced, and on reaching the Brigsteer-Kendal road turn right. Walk uphill for 100m and pass through a kissing gated sited alongside a fingerpost inscribed *Scout Scar.* Ahead lies a well-defined, broad grassy track which gently climbs the fellside towards a cairn of untidy stones. The retrospective view to the Kent estuary is outstanding especially the sea-side village of Arnside and the Kent viaduct linking Arnside with its coastal neighbour, Grange-over-Sands. Rising

above the estuary is Arnside Knott, a well-known local landmark in this part of the Lake District.

Above the cairn are two wooden gates. Proceed through the smaller of the two. The path drifts away from an accompanying wall only to run below a second wall before entering a shallow depression. The path then climbs to a gap in the scar where it joins two paths running north-south along the crest.

In windy conditions, unlike the two walkers in the photograph (page 98), it would be sensible to adopt one of the paths away from the escarpment edge. Whilst Scout Scar at an elevation of 230m is not particularly high it is exposed to gusty winds blowing straight off the Irish Sea

Lakeland cottages at Holeslack
(National Trust)

Having chosen a suitable path for the weather conditions, walk in a northerly direction passing a second cairn marking a steep path slanting down to a prominent farmhouse at the foot of the escarpment. This is <u>not</u> our route. Stay on the crest.

After passing through a gap in a roller-coaster of a limestone wall keep an eye out for the mushroom. This is not a rare fungus that grows amongst the grikes between the limestone pavements but rather the local name for a shelter built in 1912 as a memorial to George V.

The views from the shelter encompass 360 degrees taking in the Pennine hills, the Howgill fells, the Langdales, the Old Man of Coniston and when the sky is gin-clear even

Blackpool Tower.

From the mushroom take one of the paths leaning leftwards towards the escarpment edge and continue drinking in the magnificent scenery.

In April keep an eye-open for the early purple orchis recognisable by its central spike of purple flowers and green leaves with dark brown spots; these grow amongst the limestone rocks on the plateau. The rare plant is protected by law and should not be removed.

In its final stages the path drifts away from the edge of the escarpment as it descends towards the Underbarrow road. Cunswick Scar, our next objective, lies beyond the road

Walking along Scout Scar with the Lyth Valley below

If pressed for time or in adverse weather conditions the Underbarrow road provides the shortest route into Kendal. However, the short cut is inferior to the full route which, although slightly longer, maintains the quality of the walk to the end.

A kissing gate gains access to the road. On the opposite side is a car park. Enter the car park and on your right next to a notice board a path leads into a wood. Take this path which passes to the side of the telecom tower where the main woodland path is joined. Exit the wood via a gate accessing a rough downhill slopping pasture crossed by overhead power lines.

The right of way follows the power lines to the corner of a stone wall where a sign for *Cunswick Fell* is located. Turn the corner and follow the path (which now runs parallel to a stone wall on your left) for half a mile.

The limestone plateau where the rare Purple Orchis grows (Scout Scar)

The Mushroom

Rocking and rolling on Scout Scar

99

Eventually you arrive at a wooden gate. Pass through the gate and follow the path into and out of a shallow valley. Where the path forks continue due north. At the second fork take the path that makes a bee-line for the large cairn standing slightly to the right of the escarpment edge. About 100m before the cairn the path forks yet again with a path peeling away downhill towards the Kendal bypass. This is our route but before joining the path continue to the cairn where you will be rewarded with extensive views to the central Lakeland fells, the far eastern fells, High Street where the Romans built their high-level highway, and the impeccably lovely Kent Valley. This relatively low-level viewpoint (207m) ranks amongst the very finest in south-east Lakeland.

Do not stray anywhere to the west of the cairn as the cliff face along the escarpment is precipitous. Children should be closely supervised.

Retrace your steps back to where the path forks and take the left branch which leads to a second pasture. Cross this pasture and take the ladder stile leading to a limestone cutting where a footbridge unerringly spans the Kendal bypass.

Cross the bridge and take the uphill path (ignoring the other two paths on your right and left) running below a stone wall on your left. After the second pasture the path enters the northern perimeter of the Kendal Golf Club course. When safe to do so cross the fairway on the public waymarked path keeping at all times a watchful eye for aerial borne golf balls!

The well-trodden path now begins a gentle descent towards a gap where two stone walls meet at right angles. Pass through the gap and turn right. The wall marking the boundary of the golf course is on your right. Stay with the broad path as it crosses a slopping pasture dotted with wooden seats affording a bird's eye view of the *Auld Grey Town* sprawling across the Kent Valley below.

The path leads to Serpentine Wood which is popular with dog-walkers and mountain bikers. Enter the wood to the right of a stately beech tree. After a short distance the path forks. Go with the higher-level path on your right. This threads its way between magnificent beech trees.

Keep walking forward forsaking all paths leading off to your right. Ahead stands a summerhouse. Our path passes to the right of this Victorian curiosity. A garden nursery occupies lower ground below the summer house.

A little way beyond the summer house the woodland path matures into a tarmac track which exits the wood in front of a road safety barrier. Cross the road and turn right. Walk 70m downhill passing to the left of a small triangular green. Continue to follow the downhill road lined with handsome Victorian villas built of dressed limestone.

Ahead in the middle distance is an obelisk marking the site of Kendal's first motte-and-bailey castle built in 1180 (circa).

Bear left on reaching a second triangular green with a second green on the opposite side of the road.

The road bisecting the two village greens is Beast Banks (the name derives from where cattle long ago were penned prior to being slaughtered by butchers working in the Old

Shambles). The road going uphill from the two greens is Greenside and has a literary association.

Postman Pat

John Cuncliffe, the creator of Postman Pat, lived in Kendal for six years. No 10 Greenside, now a private dwellinghouse was formerly a post office which closed in 2003 and the inspiration for Mrs Goggin's Post Office in the television series and the Postman Pat books.

The former post office is about 150m up the hill on your right, just a few steps beyond the public house with a military association.

Further down the hill Beast Banks undergoes a metamorphosis to become Allhallows Lane where there once stood a medieval church. Ahead is the Town Hall which has been unkindly likened to a French railway station.

In many ways it would be fitting to end our walk in front of the Town Hall in tribute to Alfred Wainwright who worked in the building before retiring as Treasurer of Kendal Borough Council and whose pictorial guides to the Lakeland Fells have been an inspiration to generations of hill walkers ever since his first guide was published in 1955.

But this frenetically busy corner of Highgate and Lowther Street imprisoned by a notorious one-way traffic system would be something of an anti-climax.

At the corner turn right into Highgate. The main thoroughfare which runs through the heart of Kendal is divided into three sections and confusingly each section has its own name - the middle section is known as

Kendal Town Hall

Highgate, the northern end of the thoroughfare is Stricklandgate and the southern section is Kirkland meaning "church land". Kirkland is the oldest and most attractive part of Kendal and our final objective.

Walk along Highgate passing on your right Captain French Lane (easily overlooked as it is quite narrow) and Gillingate. You have now entered the old village of Kirkland. Walk down the road a little further and on your left is the parish church of Kirkland.

Resist the temptation to dive straight into the Ring O' Bells (the only public-house in England built on consecrated ground) for a well-earned celebratory drink. Enter the church grounds through the imposing heavy iron gates. The eight hundred year old church with its splendid five aisles is built on a site above the River Kent. In this graceful corner of old Kendal surrounded by lovely limestone buildings we end our walk.

HOLY TRINITY

The earliest parts of this church are 13th century although an earlier church is recorded by the Domesday Survey of 1086. Most of the fabric was built about 1400 - 1600 when the town's cloth trade was at its peak. In 1553 Queen Mary gave the living to Trinity College, Cambridge, which is still its patron. The church is the largest in Cumbria and in the 19th century regularly accommodated about 1100 people.
KENDAL CIVIC SOCIETY

Plaque erected outside the parish church

Magnificent gates leading to the parish church

Kendal parish church dating from the 13th-century

Kendal

Kendal is unquestionably the capital and principal town in the southern Lake District. It lies a mere seven miles from Lake Windermere in a favoured position in the lower reaches of the Kent Valley surrounded by low hills. It was the largest town in the old county of Westmorland before that county along with Cumberland and parts of Lancashire and Yorkshire were subsumed into the new county of Cumbria following the 1972 reorganisation. The town lies less than a mile outside the Lake District National Park boundary although the Park is administered from its head office in Kendal.

The most striking feature of Kendal is that most of its buildings are built not of slate, which is the common building material in the neighbouring towns and villages of Windermere, Bowness, Hawkshead, Ambleside and Grasmere, but limestone. The appellation "Auld Grey Town" is therefore highly appropriate.

History

The Romans built a fort at Watercrook, a strategically important crossing point on the River Kent, which lies just south of present day Kendal. Four hundred years after the Romans departed a small settlement sprung up around a Saxon church which grew into the medieval township known as Kirkland and which predates Kendal itself. For many years Kendal was known as Kirkby Kendal.

To consolidate their conquest of north-west England and in order to protect an important river crossing, the Normans hastily constructed a wooden castle of the motte-and-bailey type on a knoll overlooking the River Kent. Castle Howe, as it is known, predates by a hundred years Kendal's second, and better known, stone castle, the ruins of which stand on the opposite bank of the river. The stone castle came into the ownership of the Parr family and according to local legend Henry VIII's sixth wife, Katherine Parr, was born in the castle.

Golden Age

Kendal's golden age began in the 13th-century and lasted until the end of the 17th-century. During this period the wool trade formed the bedrock of its economy so much so that the town's motto is "wool is my bread". In the early days the wool was spun by the women of Kendal in their own homes and woven by the men folk on cottage looms. Kendal was famous for its dyes that were applied to two hardwearing wool-based cloths known as "Kendal White Spotted" and "Kendal Green". The former was worn by English bowmen at Flodden Field and the latter was mentioned by Shakespere in Henry IV Part I.

The town received its market charter in 1189 and became a natural centre where farmers and tradesmen from outlying areas would meet and conduct business. At one time up to sixty inns served the many tradespeople and travellers visiting the town. With the decline of the wool trade in the early part of 18th-century the redundant fulling mills and warehouses along the banks of the River Kent were turned into tanneries, bobbin mills and sawmills. The industrial revolution only

Kendal

lightly touched Kendal which in the 19th-century became a centre for the manufacture of snuff and shoes.

Present Day Kendal

Today tourism, the manufacture of paper and the softer IT and design based businesses form the bedrock of Kendal's economy. Culturally the town is well-served by the Kendal Museum, the Grade I listed Abbot Hall Art Gallery housing one of the finest collections of George Romney's paintings, the Brewery Arts Centre and the Museum of Lakeland Life with its permanent exhibition of books, artwork and belongings of the writer Arthur Ransome who for many years lived in the Lake District.

Highgate, Kendal

Kendal

Cobbled alleyways add to Kendal's charm

Above the banks of the River Kent

Sturdy white-washed cottages in the vernacular-style of architecture redolent of Westmorland

Appendix A

Route Maps
(numbered 1 to 25)

Key

—·—·—·—·—·—·—·—·—·—·—·—·—· Route

·· Path

—·—··—··—··—·—·—··—·— County Boundary

	Skipton to Malham	11 miles
	Malham to Settle	5.7 miles
	Settle to Clapham	7 miles
	Clapham to Ingleton	6.5 miles
	Ingleton to Kirkby Lonsdale	11.5 miles
	Kirkby Lonsdale to Levens Bridge	11.4 miles
	Levens Bridge to Kendal	9.2 miles

Important Note
Each map has been scaled individually to facilitate route navigation having regard to the nature and/or complexity of the terrain.

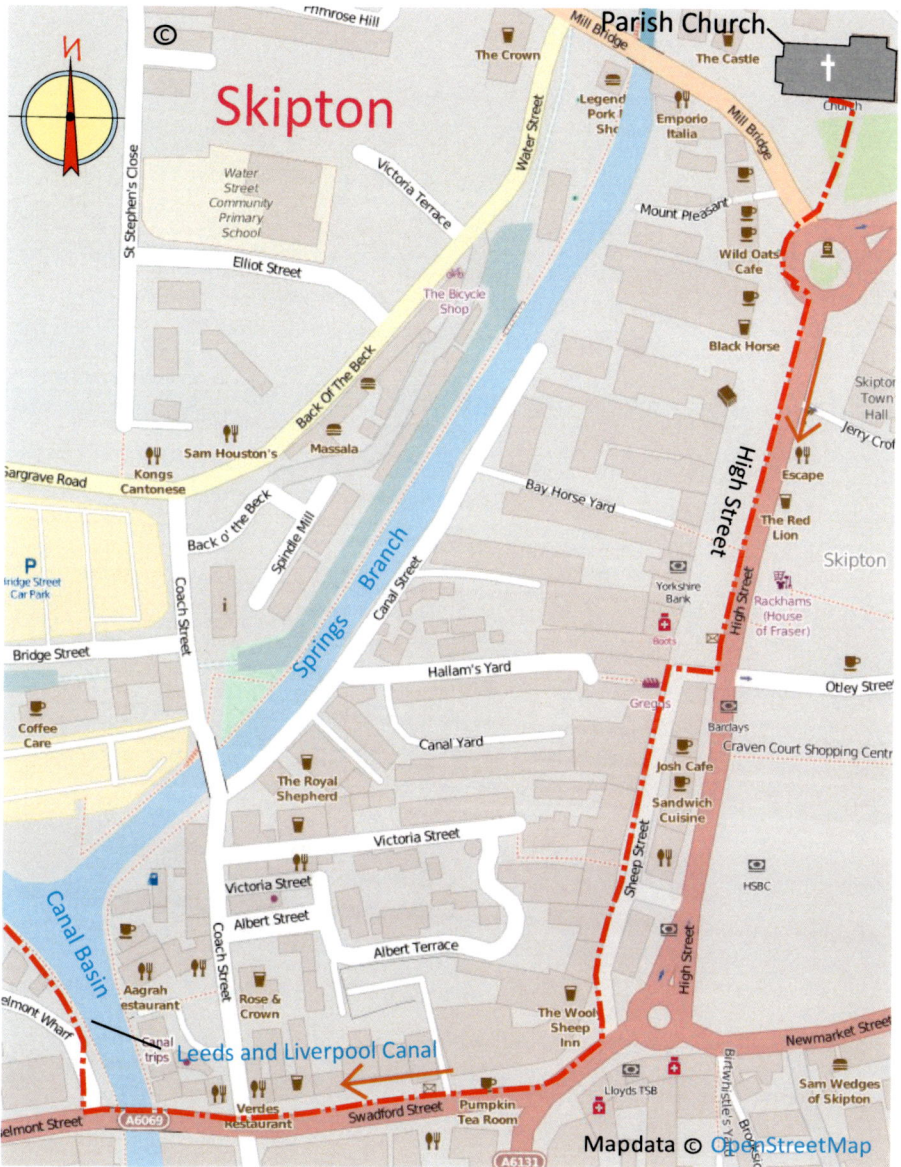

©

Skipton

Primrose Hill

The Crown

Parish Church

The Castle

Church

Water Street

Mill Bridge

Mill Bridge

Legend Pork Sho

Emporio Italia

Victoria Terrace

St Stephen's Close

Water Street Community Primary School

Elliot Street

Mount Pleasant

Wild Oats Cafe

The Bicycle Shop

Black Horse

Back Of The Beck

Skipton Town Hall

Jerry Crof

Sam Houston's

Massala

Sargrave Road

Kongs Cantonese

Back o' the Beck

Spindle Mill

Bay Horse Yard

High Street

Escape

The Red Lion

Skipton

Coach Street

Springs Branch

Canal Street

Yorkshire Bank

Rackhams (House of Fraser)

P

ridge Street Car Park

i

Boots

Bridge Street

Hallam's Yard

Greggs

Otley Stree

Barclays

Coffee Care

Canal Yard

Craven Court Shopping Centr

The Royal Shepherd

Josh Cafe

Sheep Street

HSBC

Victoria Street

Sandwich Cuisine

Victoria Street

Albert Street

Coach Street

Albert Terrace

Canal Basin

elmont Wharf

Aagrah restaurant

Rose & Crown

High Street

The Wool Sheep Inn

Newmarket Stree

Canal trips

Leeds and Liverpool Canal

Verdes Restaurant

Swadford Street

Pumpkin Tea Room

Lloyds TSB

Sam Wedges of Skipton

elmont Street

A6069

Birtwhistle's

Bro

A6131

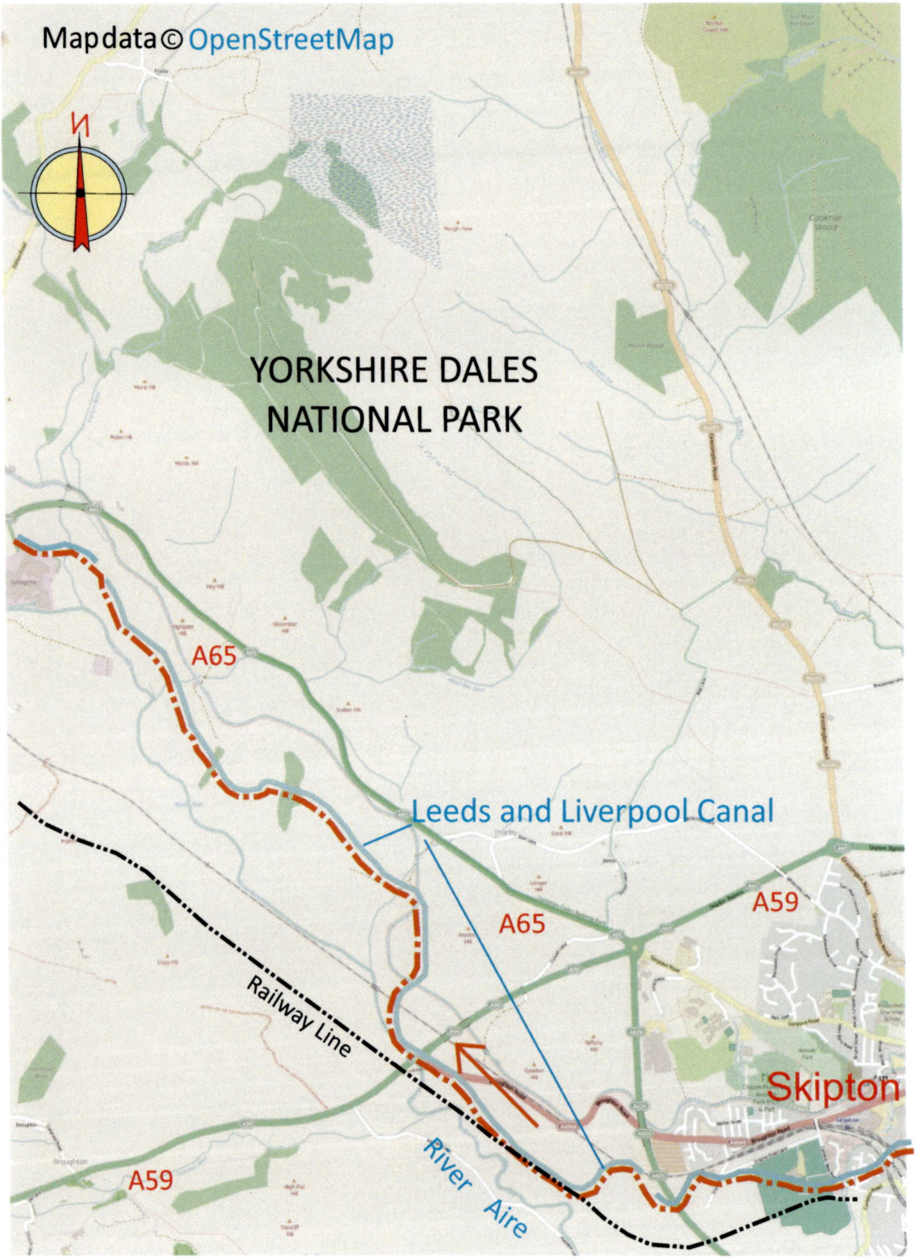

Mapdata© OpenStreetMap

YORKSHIRE DALES
NATIONAL PARK

A65

Leeds and Liverpool Canal

A65

A59

Railway Line

Skipton

A59

River Aire

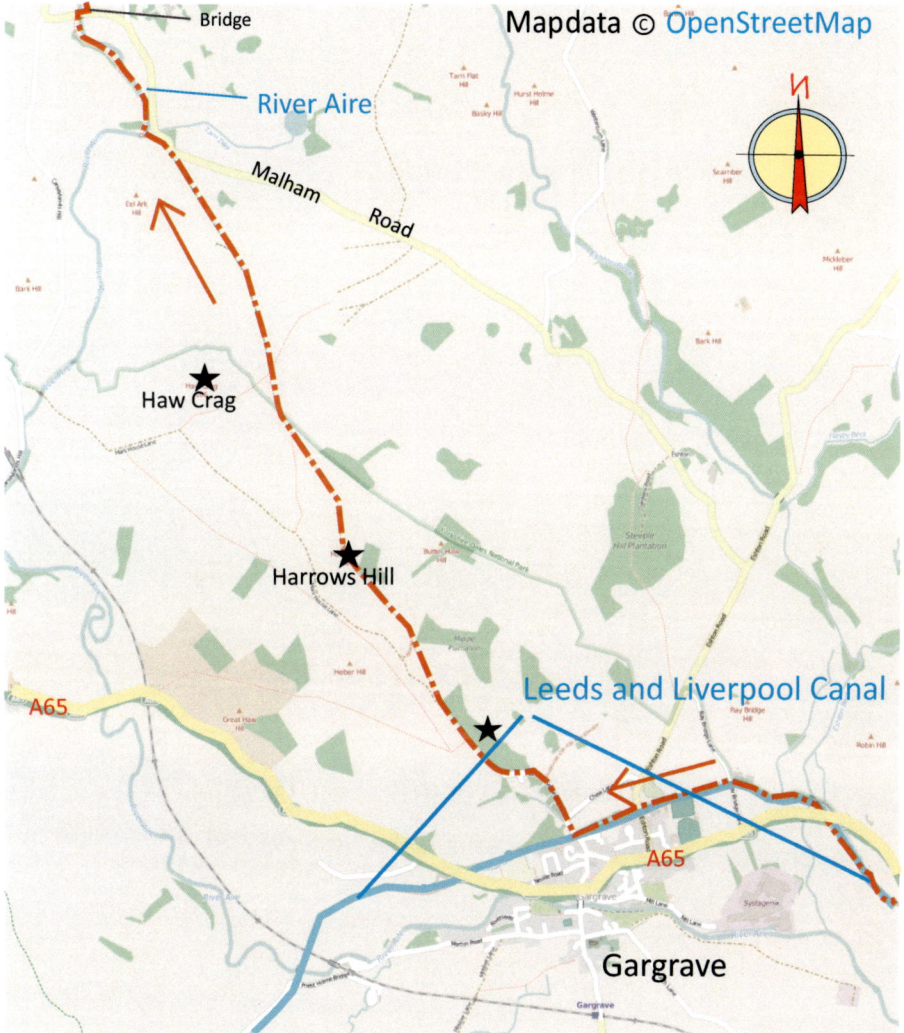

Bridge

Mapdata © OpenStreetMap

River Aire

Malham Road

Haw Crag

Harrows Hill

Leeds and Liverpool Canal

A65

A65

Gargrave

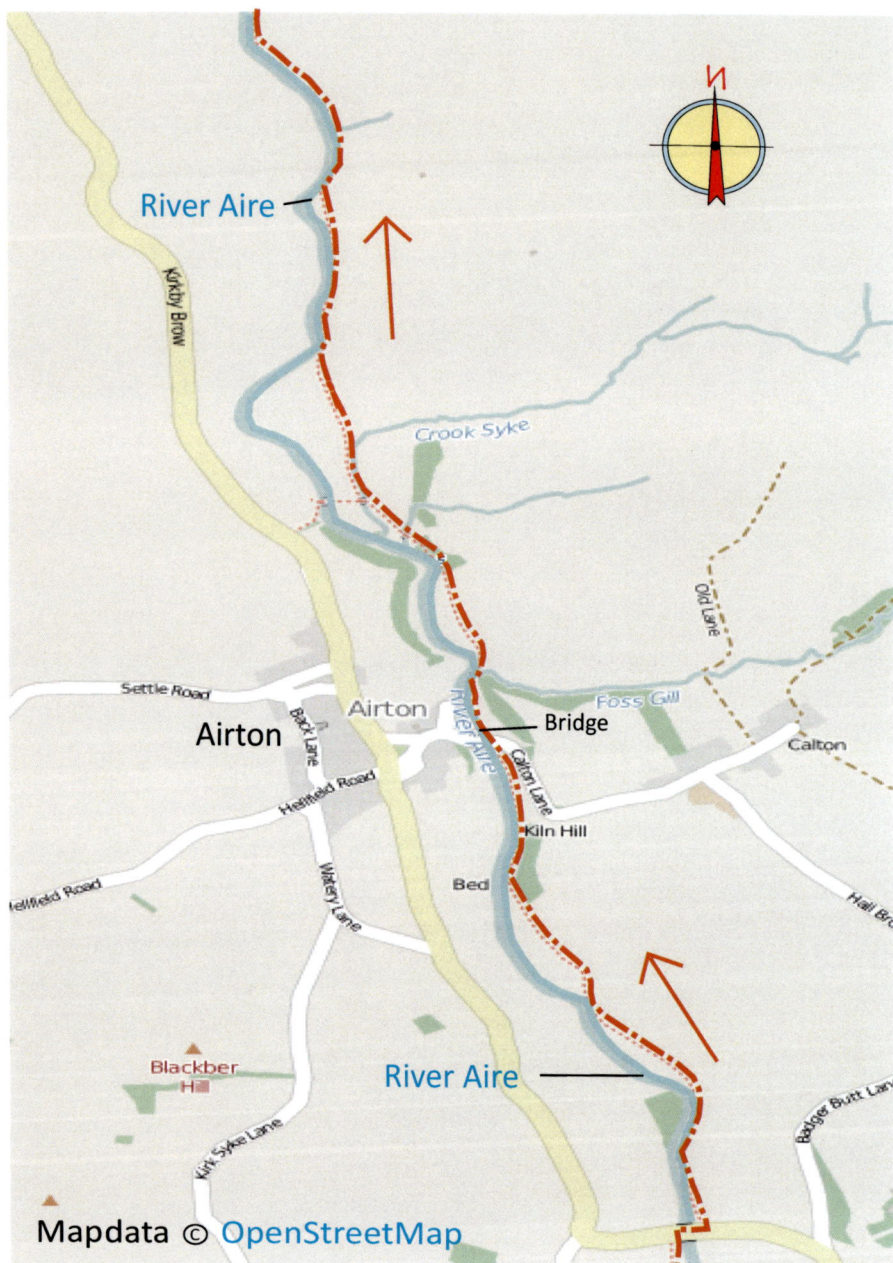

River Aire

Kirkby Brow

Crook Syke

Settle Road

Airton

Airton

Back Lane

Hellifield Road

Hellifield Road

Wakley Lane

River Aire

Bridge

Foss Gill

Calton Lane

Calton

Kiln Hill

Bed

Hall Brow

Blackber H

River Aire

Kirk Syke Lane

Badger Butt Lane

Mapdata © OpenStreetMap

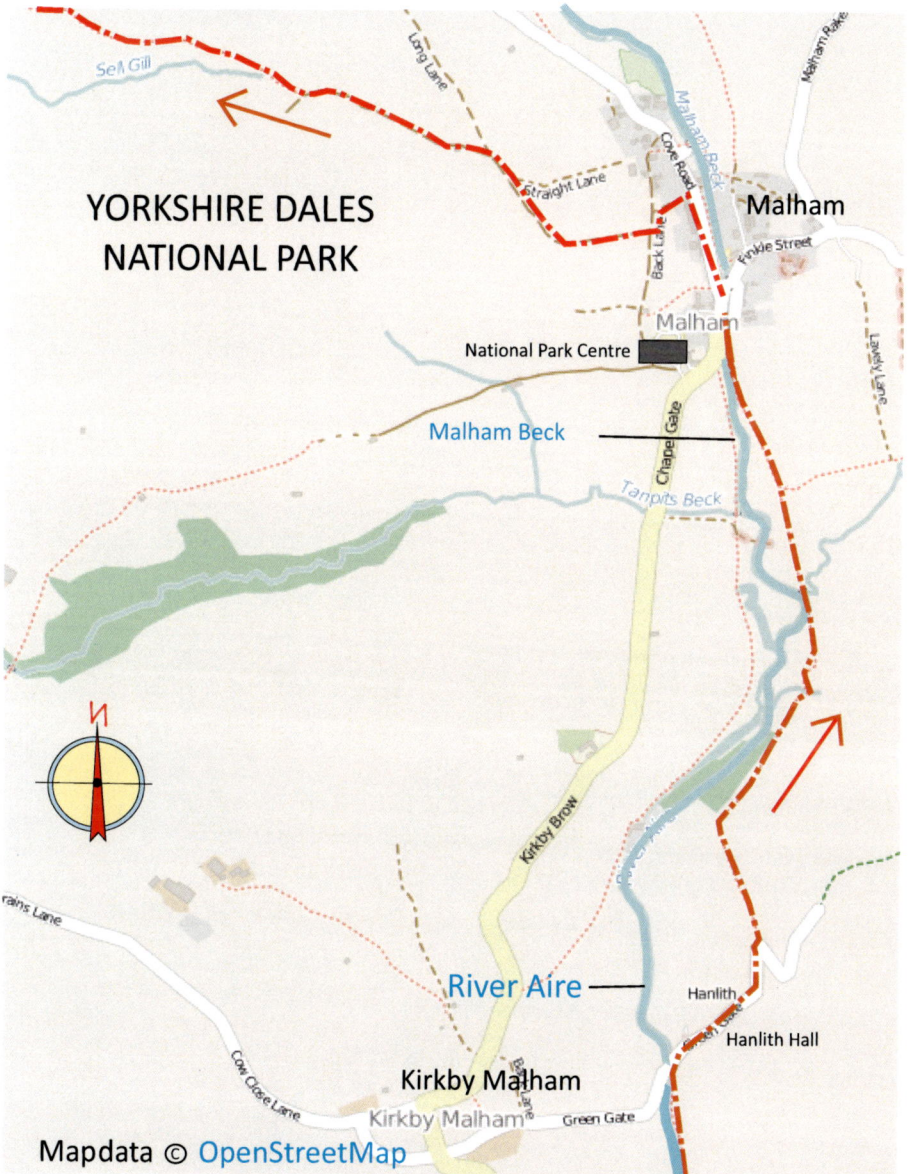

YORKSHIRE DALES
NATIONAL PARK

Malham

Sell Gill

Long Lane

Malham Rake

Cove Road

Straight Lane

Back Lane

Malham Beck

Finkle Street

Malham

National Park Centre

Malham Beck

Chapel Gate

Landyke Lane

Tanpits Beck

Kirkby Brow

Cove Lane

River Aire

Hanlith

Hanlith Hall

Grains Lane

Cove Close Lane

Kirkby Malham

Kirkby Malham

Green Gate

Green Gate

Mapdata © OpenStreetMap

Map 7

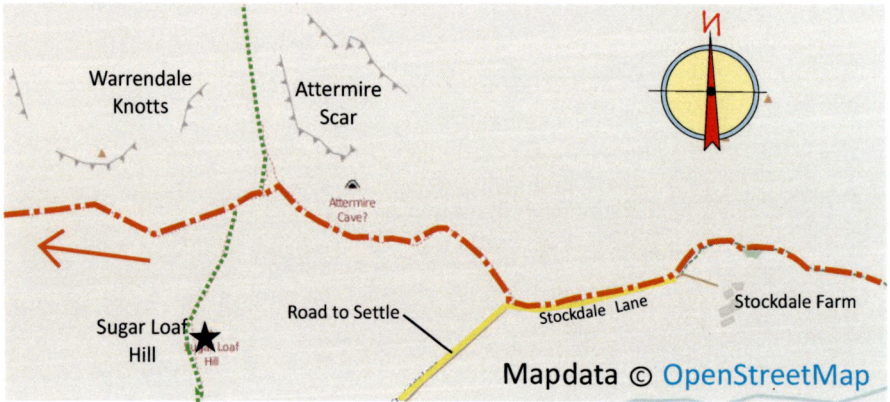

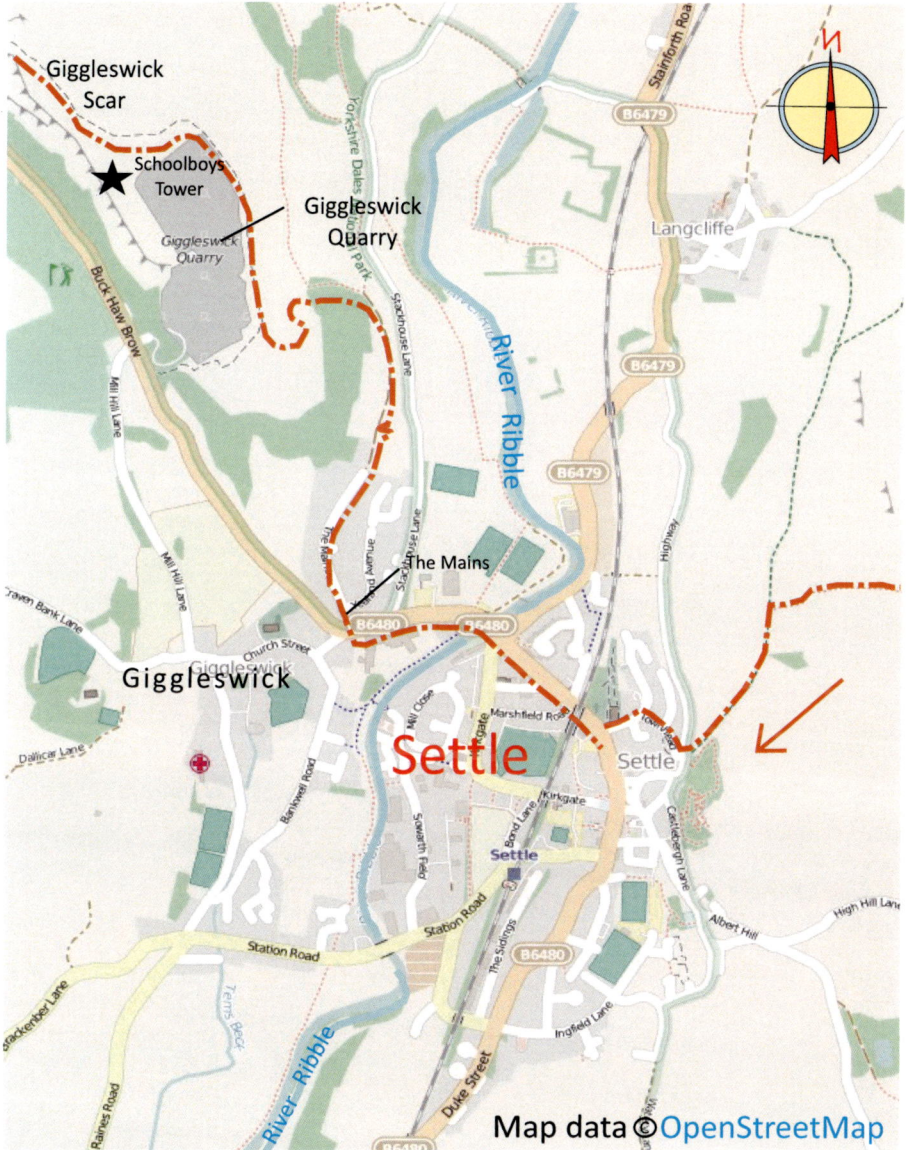

Giggleswick
Scar

Schoolboys
Tower

Giggleswick
Quarry

Giggleswick
Quarry

Langcliffe

River Ribble

B6479

B6479

B6479

Buck Haw Brow

Mill Hill Lane

Yorkshire Dales National Park

Stackhouse Lane

The Mains

B6480

B6480

Craven Bank Lane

Mill Hill Lane

Church Street

Giggleswick

Gigleswick

Marshfield Road

Settle

Settle

Dallicar Lane

Banwell Road

Mill Close

Kirkgate

Bond Lane

Settle

Sowarth Field

Castlebergh Lane

Albert Hill

High Hill Lane

Station Road

Station Road

The Sidings

B6480

Ingfield Lane

Stackenber Lane

Terns Beck

Raines Road

River Ribble

Duke Street

B6480

Stainforth Road

Highway

Map data ©OpenStreetMap

Feizor
Wood

Feizor Nick

Feizor Hill Lane

Feizor

Feizor

Kiln Hill Lane

Water Splash

**YORKSHIRE DALES
NATIONAL PARK**

Brunton Road

Dead Man's
Cave

Buck Haw Brow

Fen Beck

B6480

Yorkshire Dales National park

A65

Giggleswick Scar

B6480

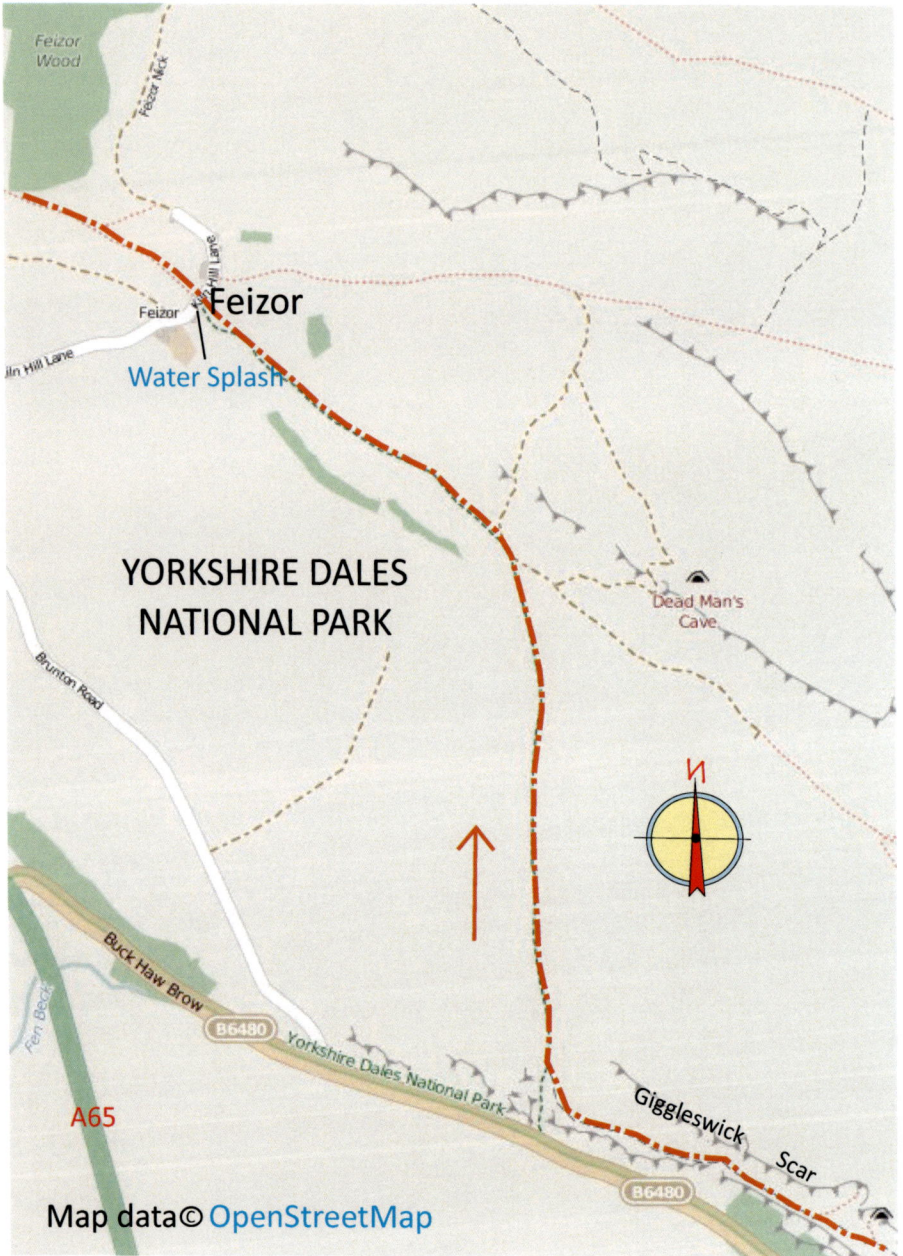

Map data© OpenStreetMap

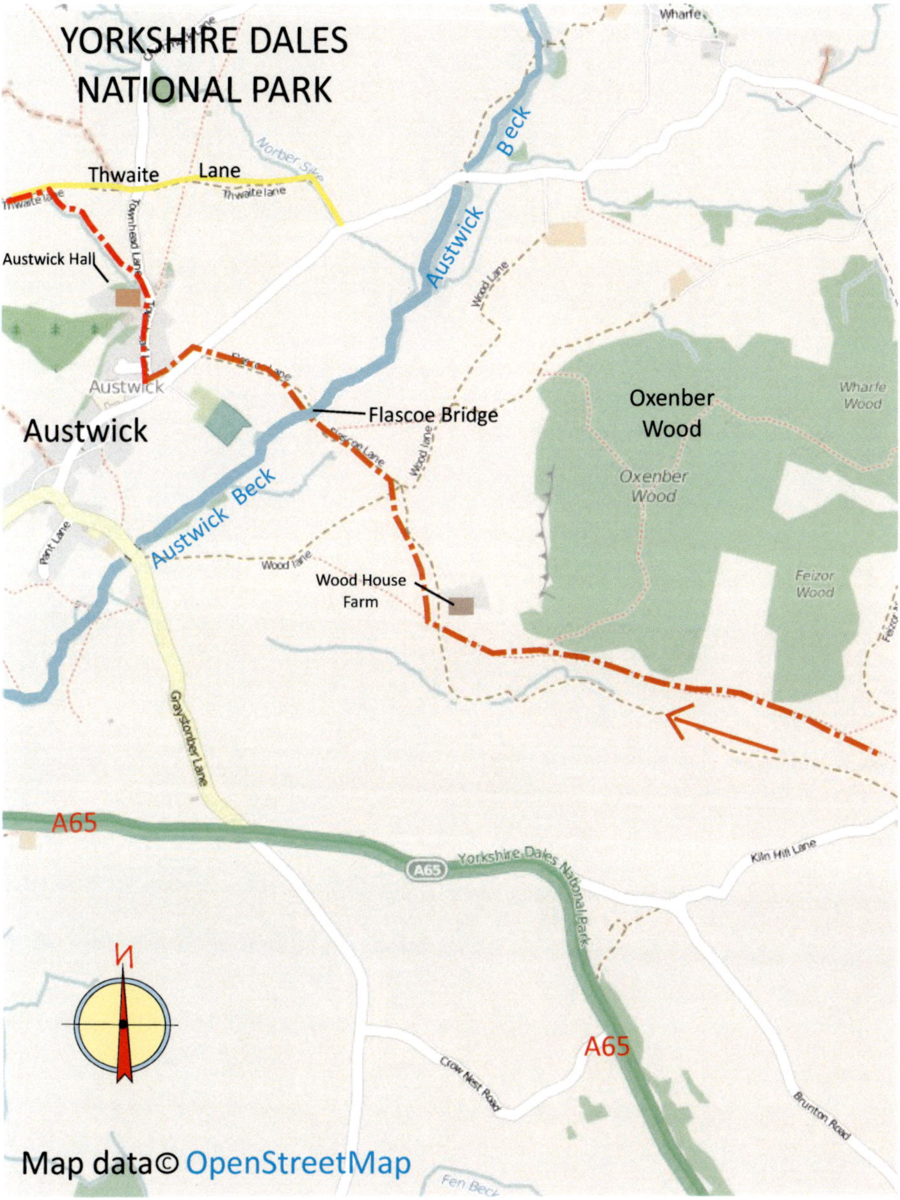
YORKSHIRE DALES
NATIONAL PARK
Thwaite Lane
Thwaite lane
Townhead Lane
Austwick Hall
Austwick
Austwick
Beck
Austwick
Austwick Beck
Flascoe Bridge
Feizor Lane
Wood Lane
Wood lane
Pant Lane
Wood House
Farm
Oxenber
Wood
Oxenber
Wood
Wharfe
Wood
Feizor
Wood
Wharfe
Norber Sike
Graystonber Lane
A65
A65
Yorkshire Dales National Park
Kiln Hill Lane
A65
Crow Nest Road
Brunton Road
Fen Beck
N
Map data© OpenStreetMap

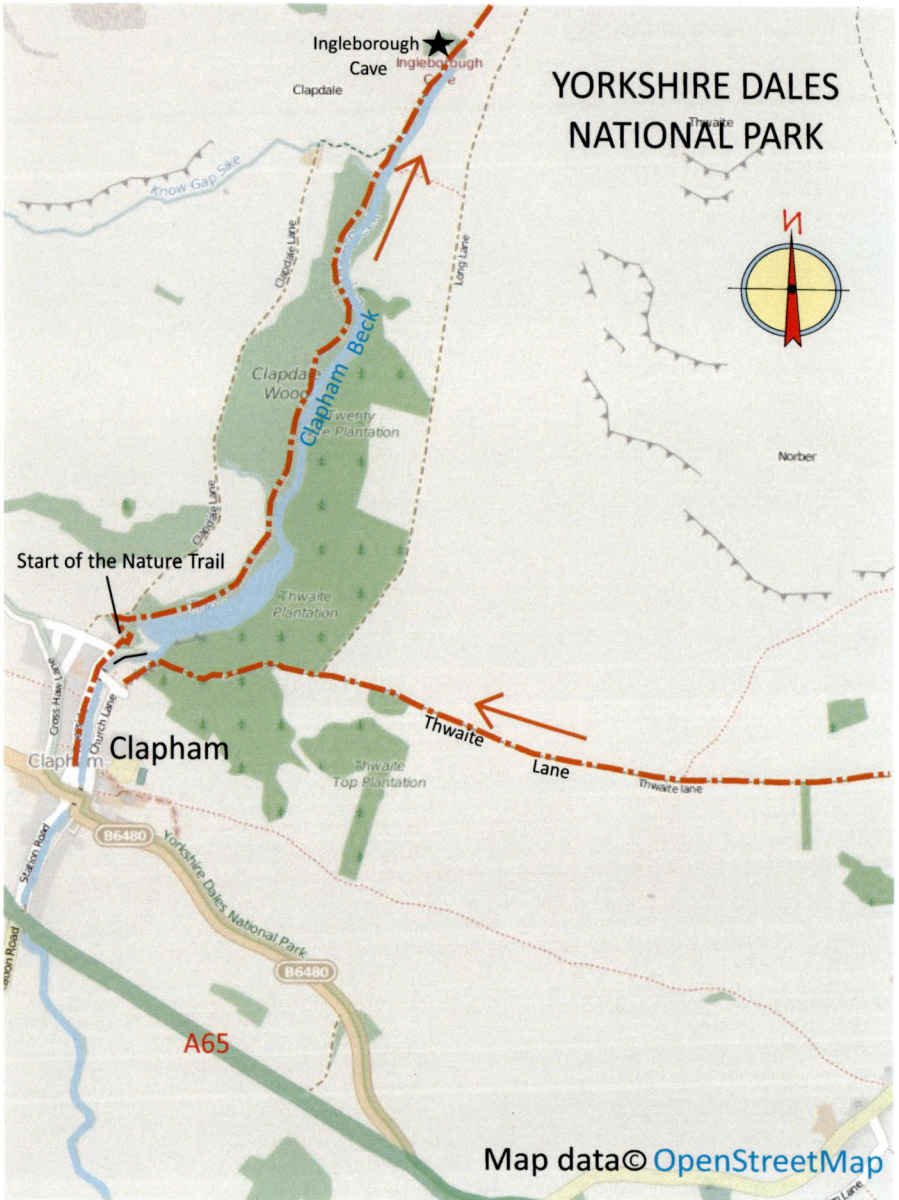

Ingleborough Cave

Clapdale

Ingleborough Cave

Clapdale

YORKSHIRE DALES NATIONAL PARK

Thwaite

Know Gap Sike

Cladgale Lane

Long Lane

Clapham Beck

Clapdale Wood

Twenty Plantation

Norber

Clapdale Lane

Start of the Nature Trail

Thwaite Plantation

Cross Haw Lane

Church Lane

Clapham

Thwaite Lane

Thwaite Lane

Clapham

Station Road

B6480

Yorkshire Dales National Park

Thwaite Top Plantation

B6480

A65

Map data© OpenStreetMap

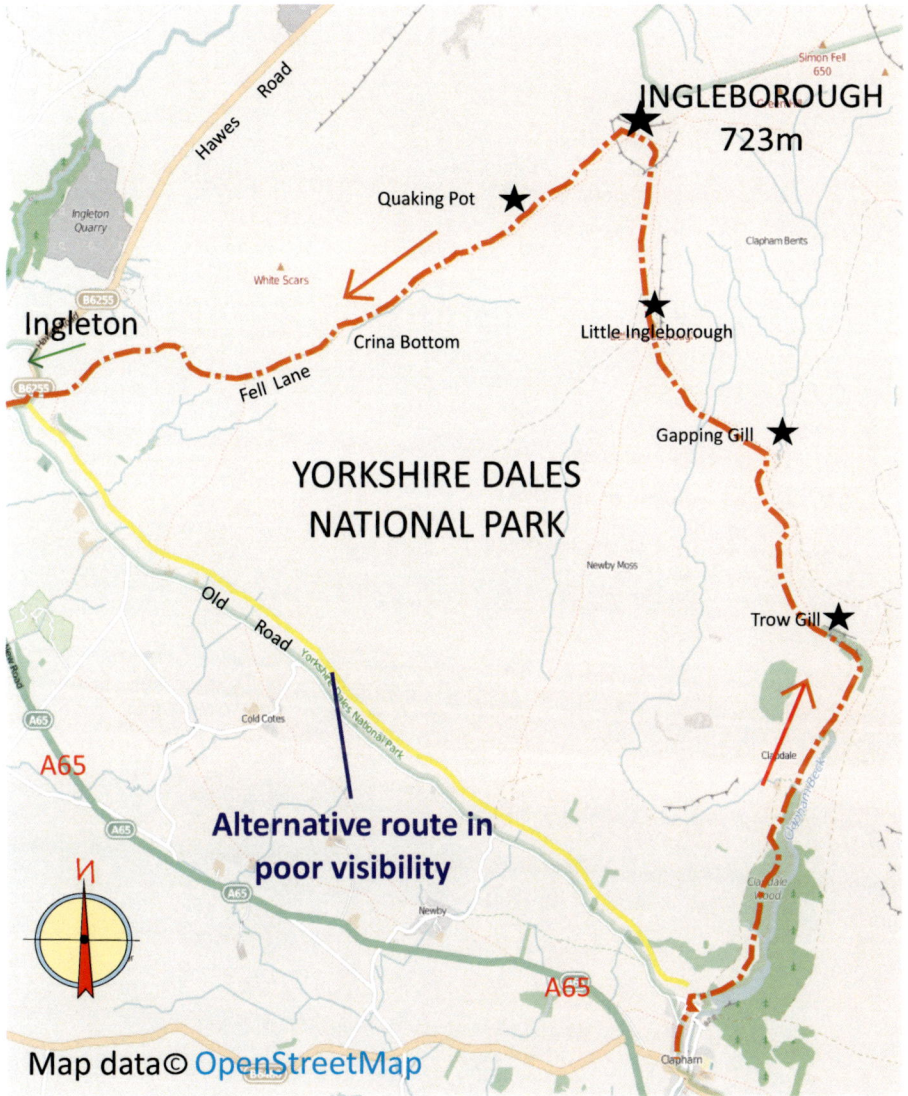

Hawes   Road

INGLEBOROUGH
723m

Simon Fell
650

Ingleton
Quarry

Quaking Pot ★

White Scars

Clapham Bents

B6255

Ingleton

Crina Bottom

Little Ingleborough ★

Fell Lane

B6255

YORKSHIRE DALES
NATIONAL PARK

Gapping Gill ★

Newby Moss

Old   Road

Yorkshire Dales National Park

Trow Gill ★

Clapdale

A65

Cold Cotes

Alternative route in
poor visibility

A65

Newby

Cold Dale
Wood

A65

Map data© OpenStreetMap

Clapham

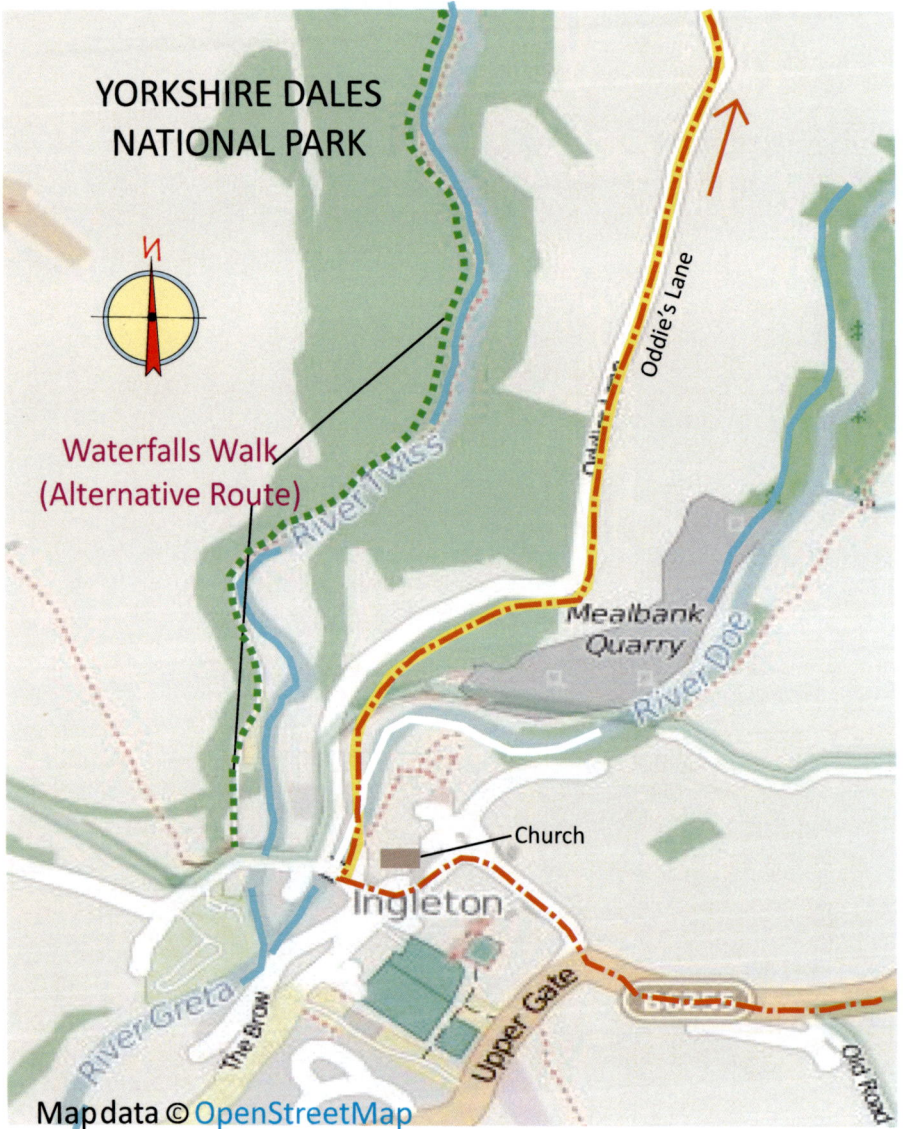

YORKSHIRE DALES
NATIONAL PARK

Waterfalls Walk
(Alternative Route)

Oddie's Lane

River Twiss

Mealbank
Quarry

River Doe

Church

Ingleton

River Greta

The Brow

Upper Gate

B6255

Old Road

Mapdata © OpenStreetMap

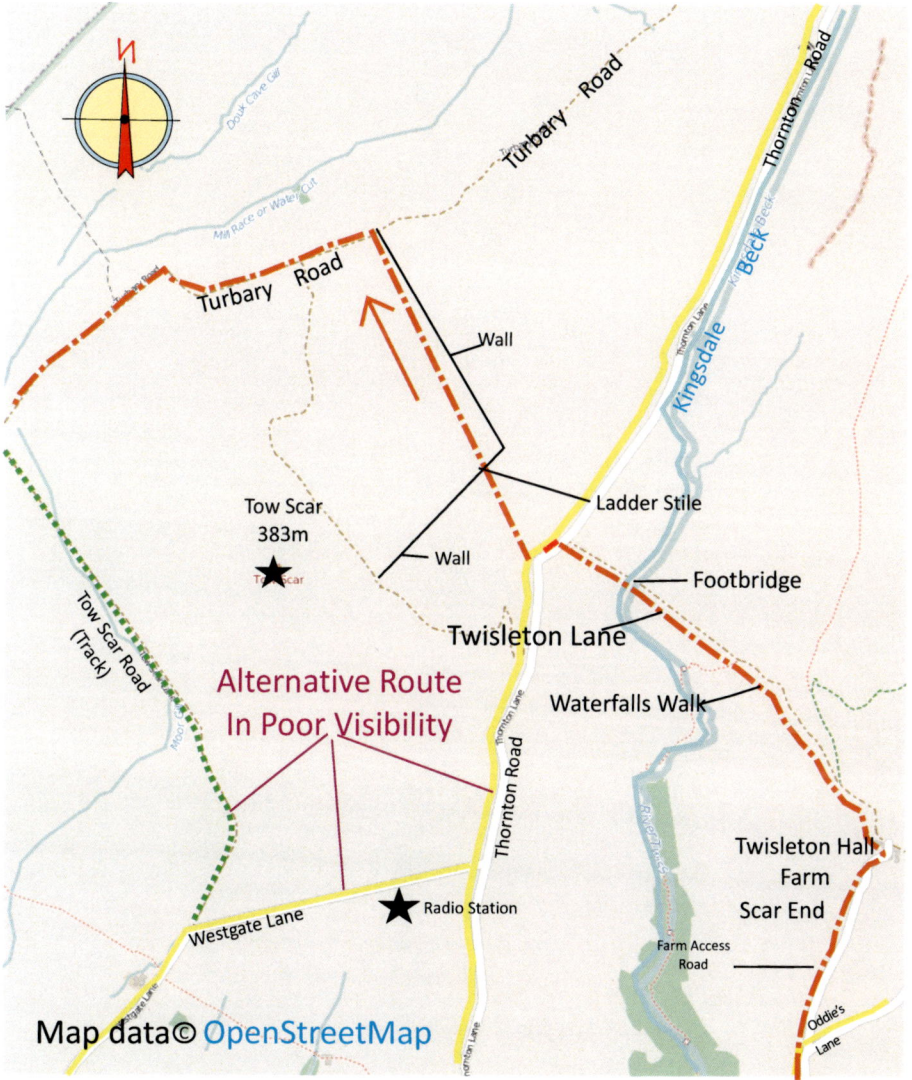

Map 14

Thornton Road

Turbary Road

Turbary Road

Wall

Kingsdale Beck

Thornton Lane

Ladder Stile

Tow Scar
383m
Tow Scar

Wall

Footbridge

Twisleton Lane

Alternative Route
In Poor Visibility

Waterfalls Walk

Thornton Road

Tow Scar Road
(Track)

Twisleton Hall
Farm
Scar End

Westgate Lane

Radio Station

Farm Access
Road

Map data© OpenStreetMap

Oddie's
Lane

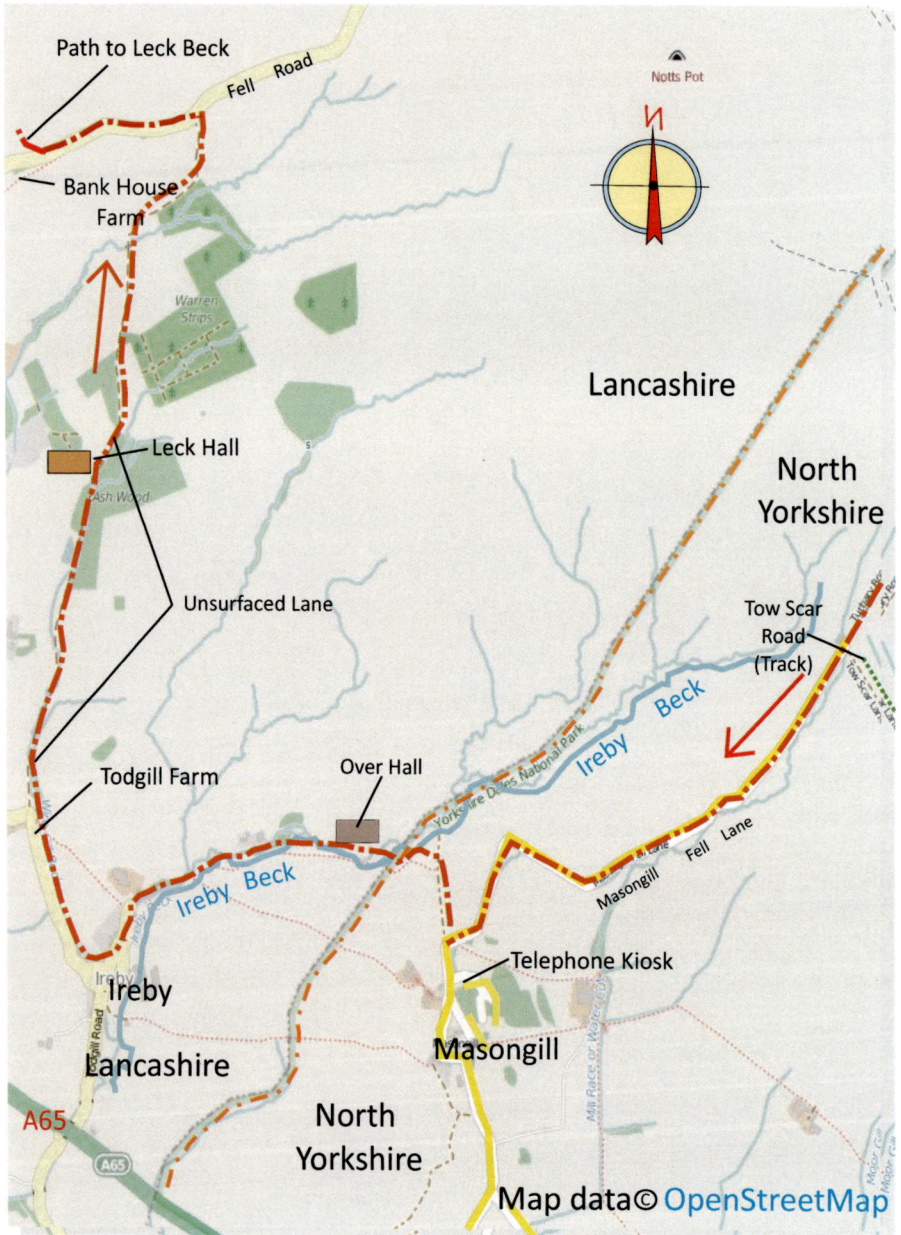

Path to Leck Beck

Fell Road

Notts Pot

Bank House
Farm

Warren
Strips

Lancashire

North
Yorkshire

Leck Hall

Ash Wood

Tow Scar
Road
(Track)

Unsurfaced Lane

Beck

Ireby Beck

Todgill Farm

Over Hall

Masongill Fell Lane

Ireby Beck

Ireby

Telephone Kiosk

Ireby

Lancashire

Masongill

A65

North
Yorkshire

Map data© OpenStreetMap

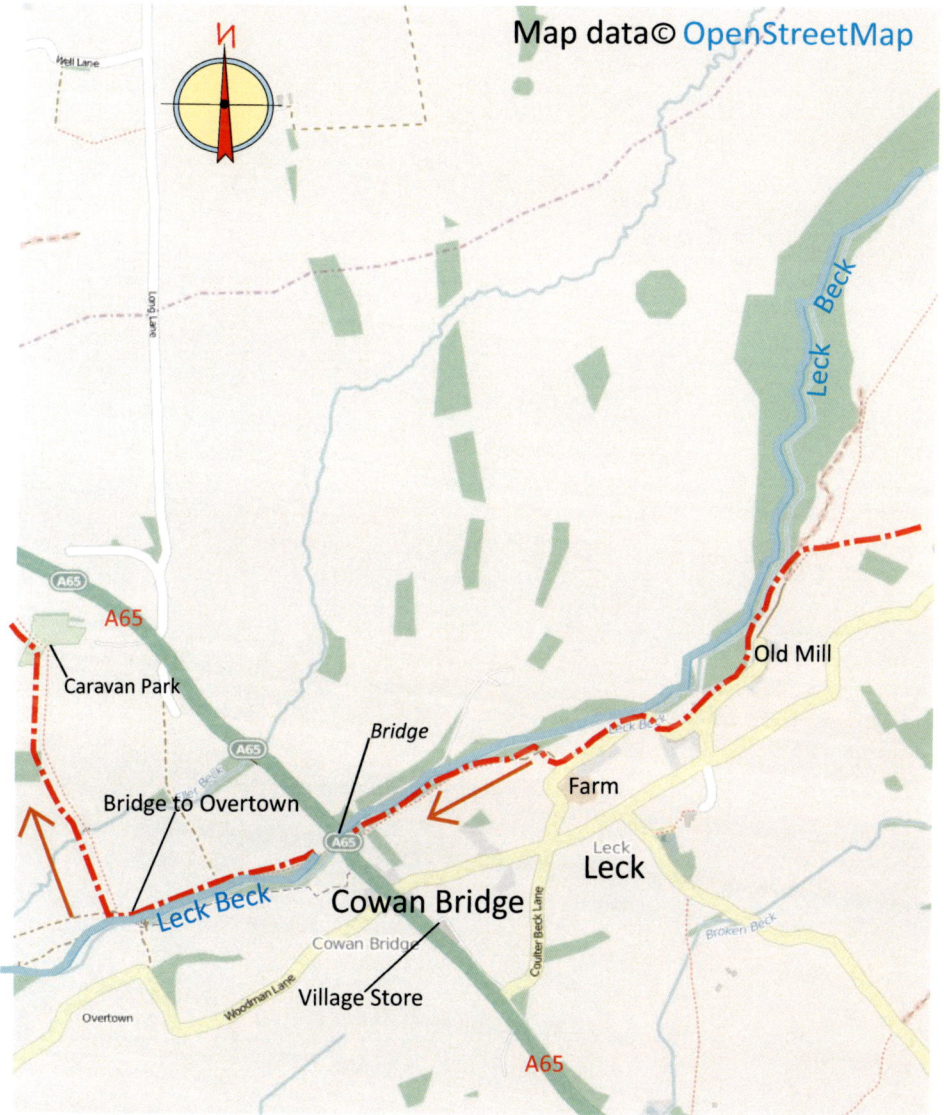

Map data© OpenStreetMap

Well Lane

Long Lane

A65

A65

Caravan Park

A65

Bridge

Bridge to Overtown

A65

Leck Beck

Old Mill

Farm

Leck

Cowan Bridge

Cowan Bridge

Coulter Beck Lane

Broken Beck

Village Store

Overtown

Woodman Lane

A65

Leck Beck

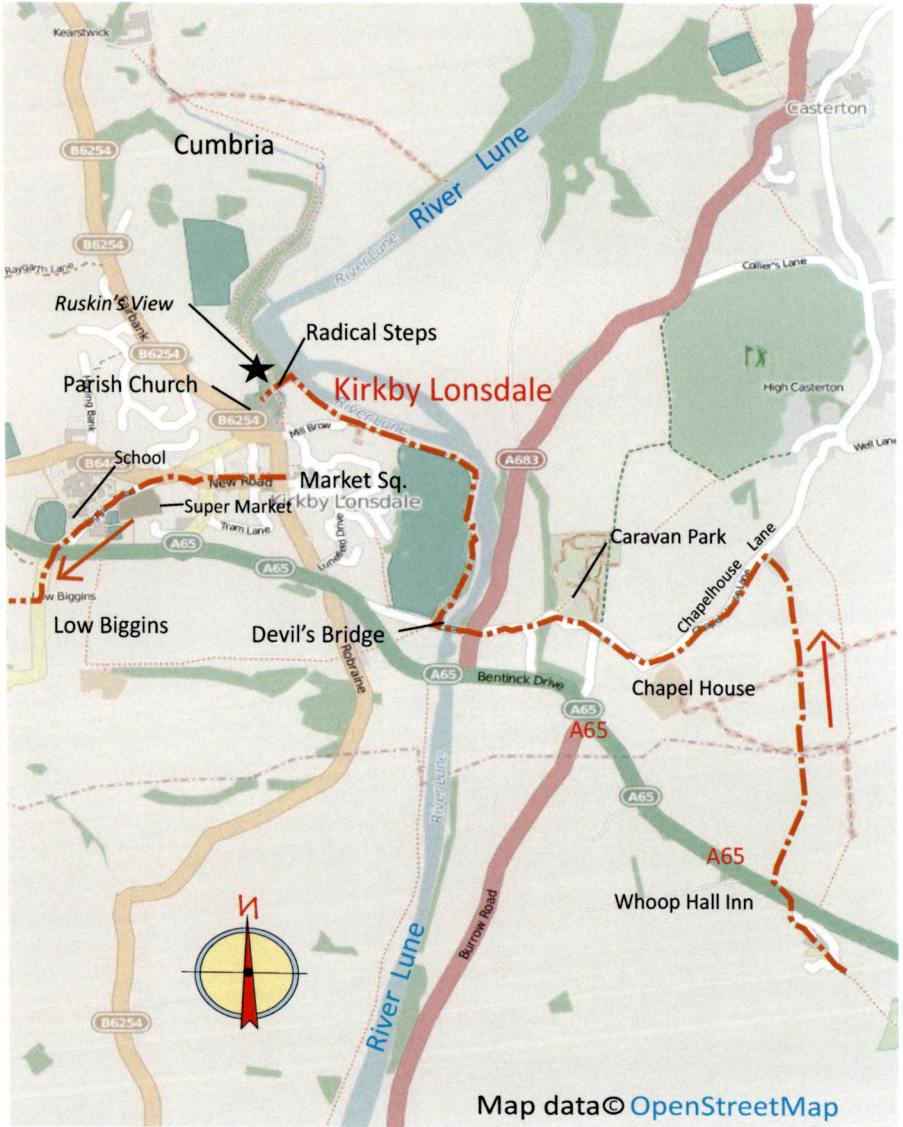

Cumbria

River Lune

B6254

Ruskin's View

Radical Steps

Parish Church

Kirkby Lonsdale

School

New Road

Market Sq.

Super Market

Caravan Park

Low Biggins

Devil's Bridge

Chapelhouse Lane

Chapel House

A65

A65

Whoop Hall Inn

River Lune

Map data© OpenStreetMap

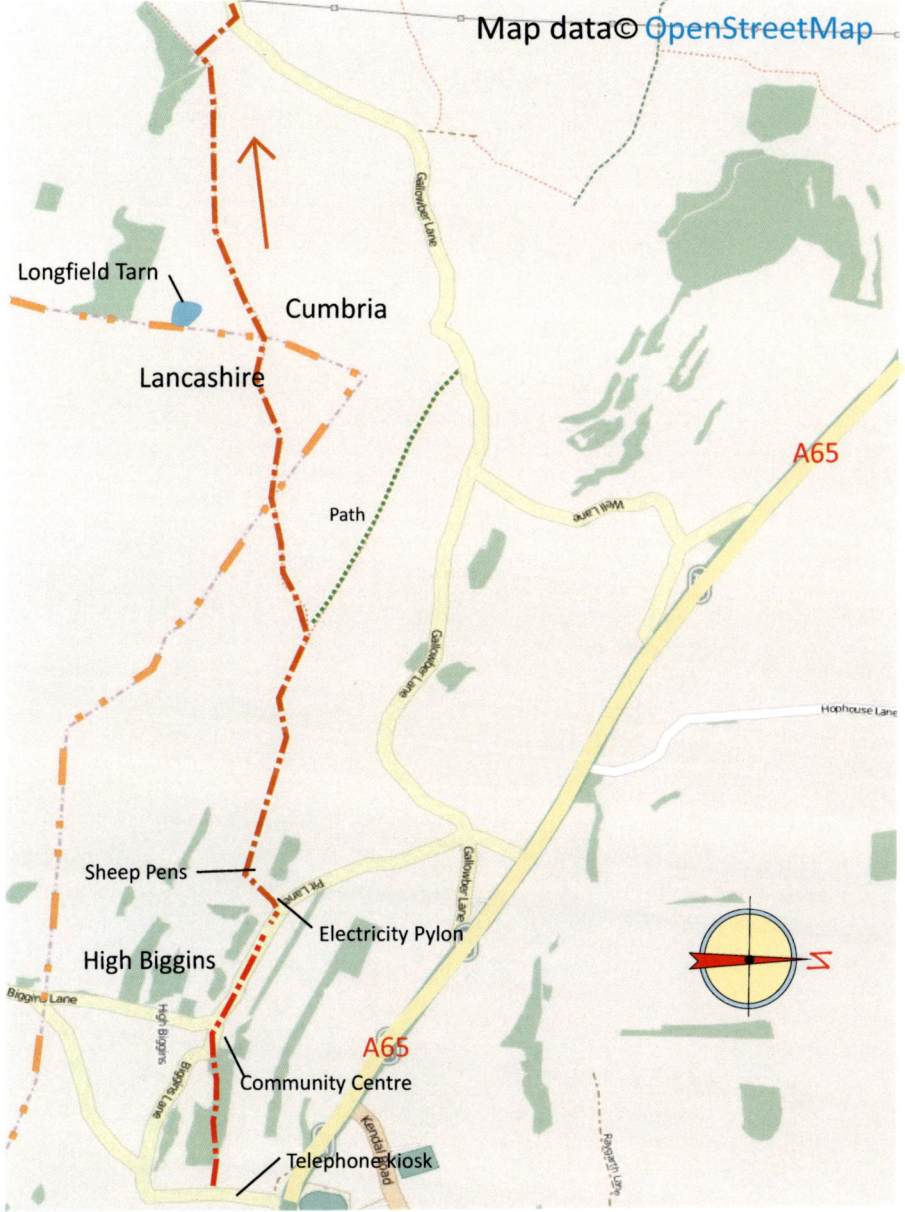

Map data© OpenStreetMap

Longfield Tarn

Cumbria

Lancashire

Gallowber Lane

A65

Path

Well Lane

Gallfields Lane

Hophouse Lane

Sheep Pens

Pit Lane

Electricity Pylon

Gallowber Lane

High Biggins

Biggins Lane

High Biggins Lane

A65

Community Centre

Kendal Head

Telephone kiosk

Fingerth Lane

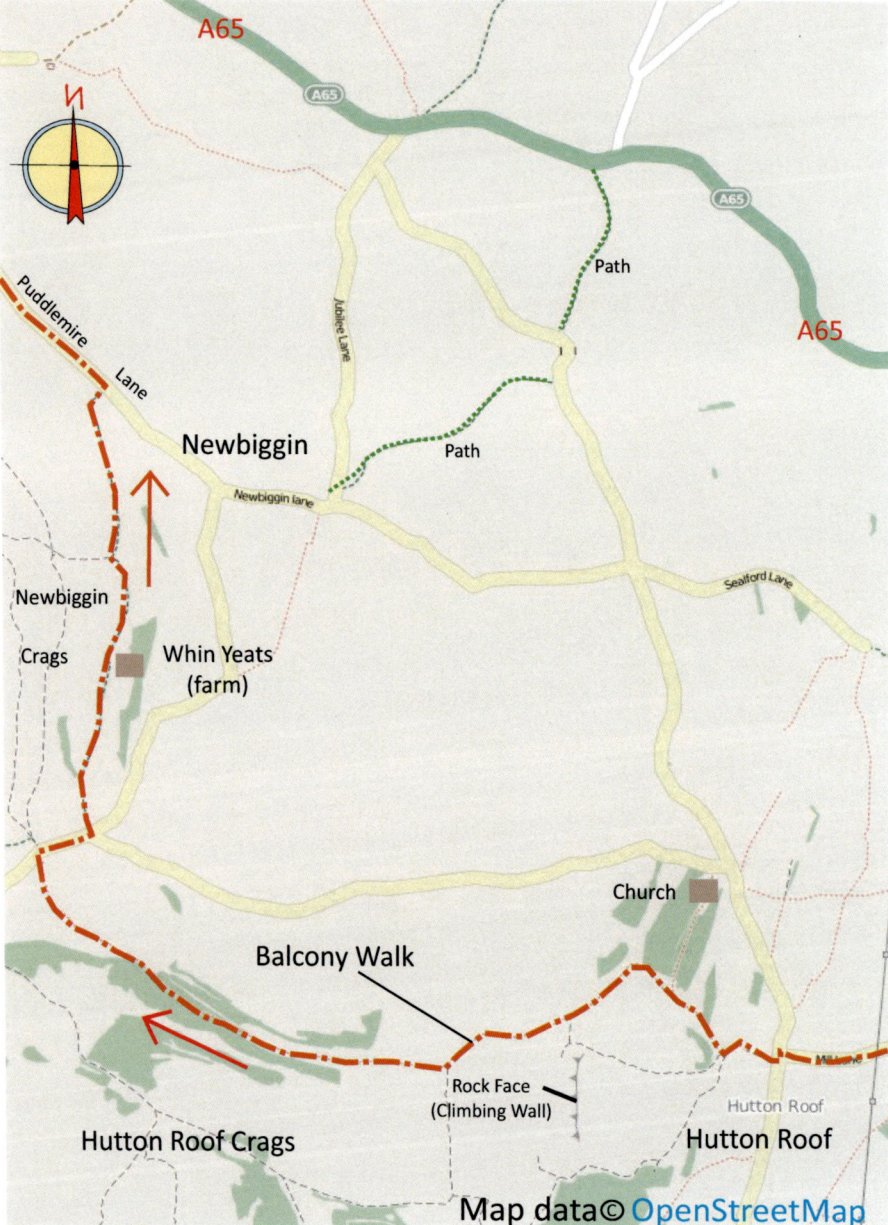

A65

A65

A65

A65

Puddlemire Lane

Path

Jubilee Lane

Newbiggin

Path

Newbiggin lane

Sealford Lane

Newbiggin
Crags

Whin Yeats
(farm)

Church

Balcony Walk

Hutton Roof Crags

Rock Face
(Climbing Wall)

Hutton Roof

Hutton Roof

Map data© OpenStreetMap

Map data© OpenStreetMap

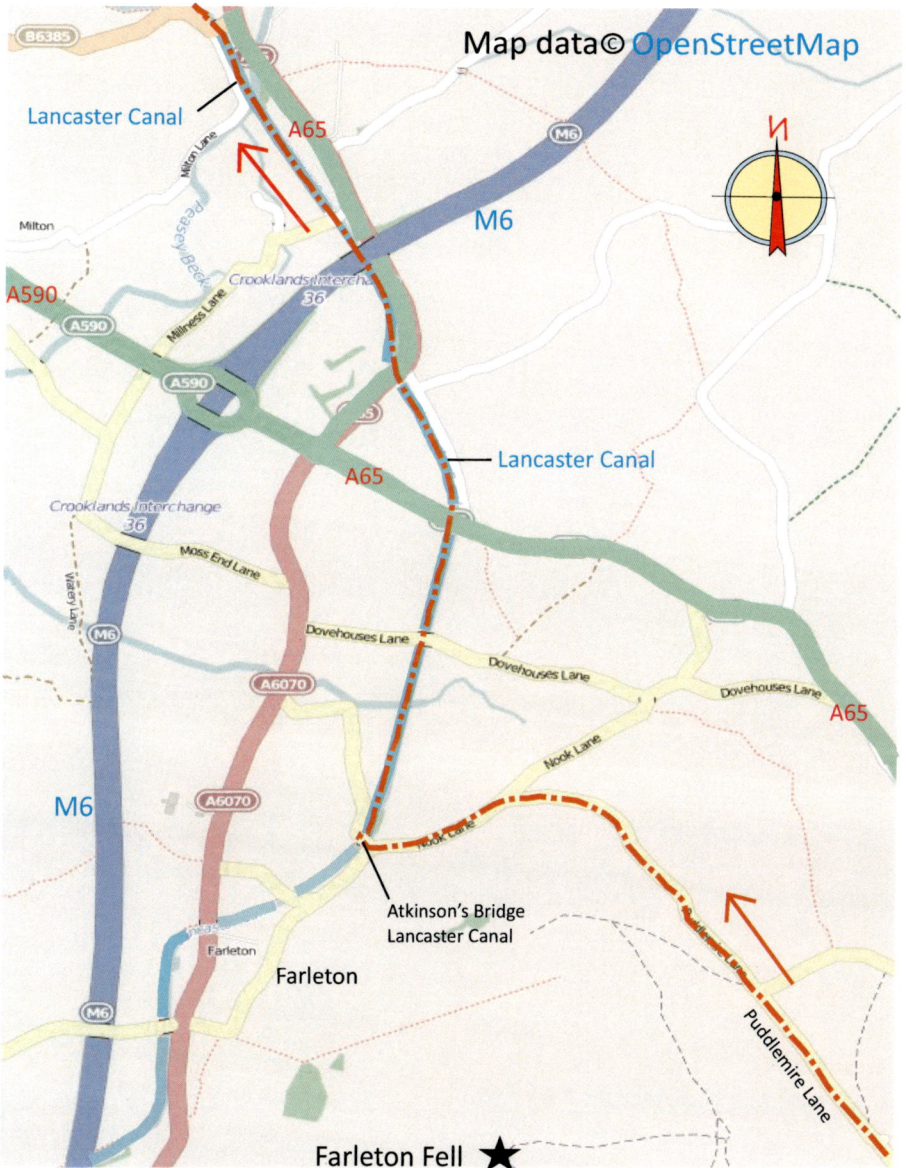

B6385

Lancaster Canal

A65

Milton Lane

M6

Milton

M6

Peasey Beck

A590

Crooklands Interch.

36

A590

Milness Lane

A590

Lancaster Canal

A65

Crooklands Interchange

36

Moss End Lane

Waery Lane

M6

Dovehouses Lane

Dovehouses Lane

Dovehouses Lane

A6070

A65

Nook Lane

M6

A6070

Nook Lane

Atkinson's Bridge
Lancaster Canal

Farleton

Farleton

M6

Puddlemire Lane

Farleton Fell ★

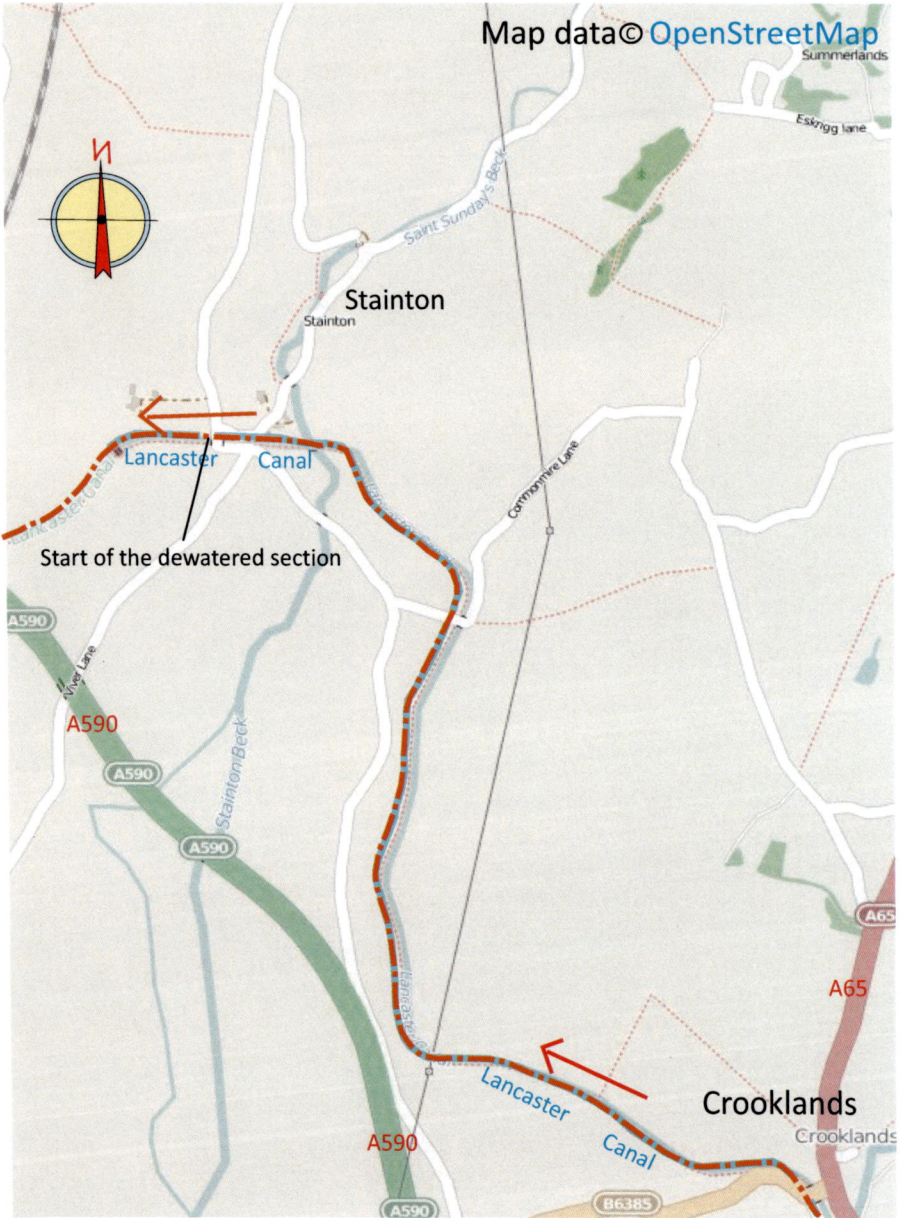

Map data© OpenStreetMap

Summerlands

Eskrigg lane

Saint Sunday's Beck

Stainton
Stainton

Lancaster Canal

Lancaster Canal

Start of the dewatered section

Cotmonshire Lane

A590

Vivey Lane

A590

A590

Stainton Beck

A590

A65

A65

Lancaster Canal

Crooklands
Crooklands

A590

B6385

A591

A591

Nannypie Lane

River Kent

Lancaster Canal

Sedgwick

Sedgwick

Brettargh Holt

A590

A590

A590

A590

A590

A590

Back Lane

Back Lane

Close

Heaves Hotel

Park Head

A590

Kent

A6

Lancaster Canal

Well Heads Lane

Lawrence
House
Plantation

River Kent

A590

A590

West Coast Main

A6

Levens Park

A590

590

Lancaster Canal

Hincaster Tunnel

West Coast Main

Well Heads Lane

Levens Bridge

Levens Bridge

Levens
Hall

A6

A6

A590

Hincaster

Hincaster Hall

Harry Brow

Hincaster Well Heads Lane

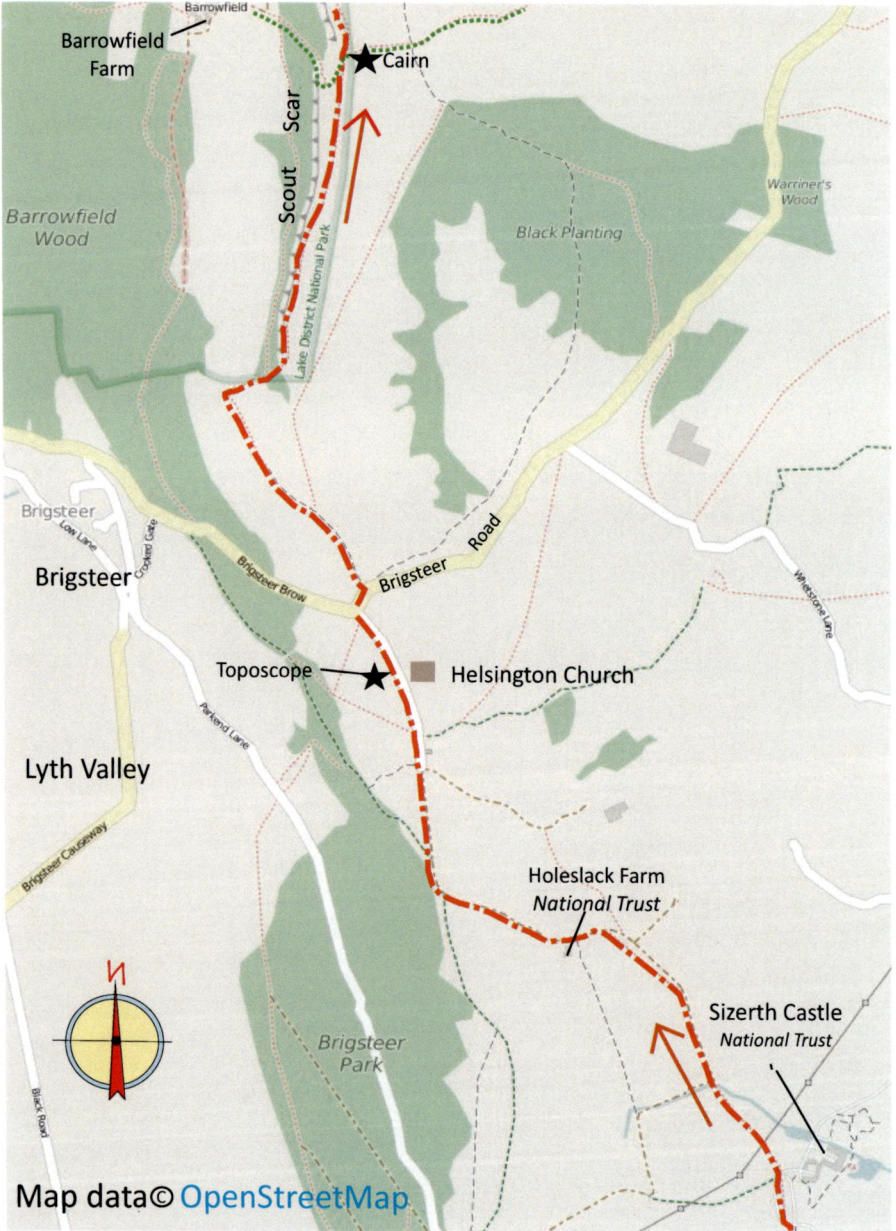

Barrowfield

Barrowfield
Farm

Scout Scar

★ Cairn

Lake District National Park

Barrowfield
Wood

Warriner's
Wood

Black Planting

Brigsteer

Low Lane

Crooked Gate

Brigsteer Brow

Brigsteer Road

Brigsteer

Whitestone Lane

Toposcope ★ ▢ **Helsington Church**

Parkend Lane

Lyth Valley

Brigsteer Causeway

Black Road

Brigsteer
Park

Holeslack Farm
National Trust

Sizerth Castle
National Trust

Map data© OpenStreetMap

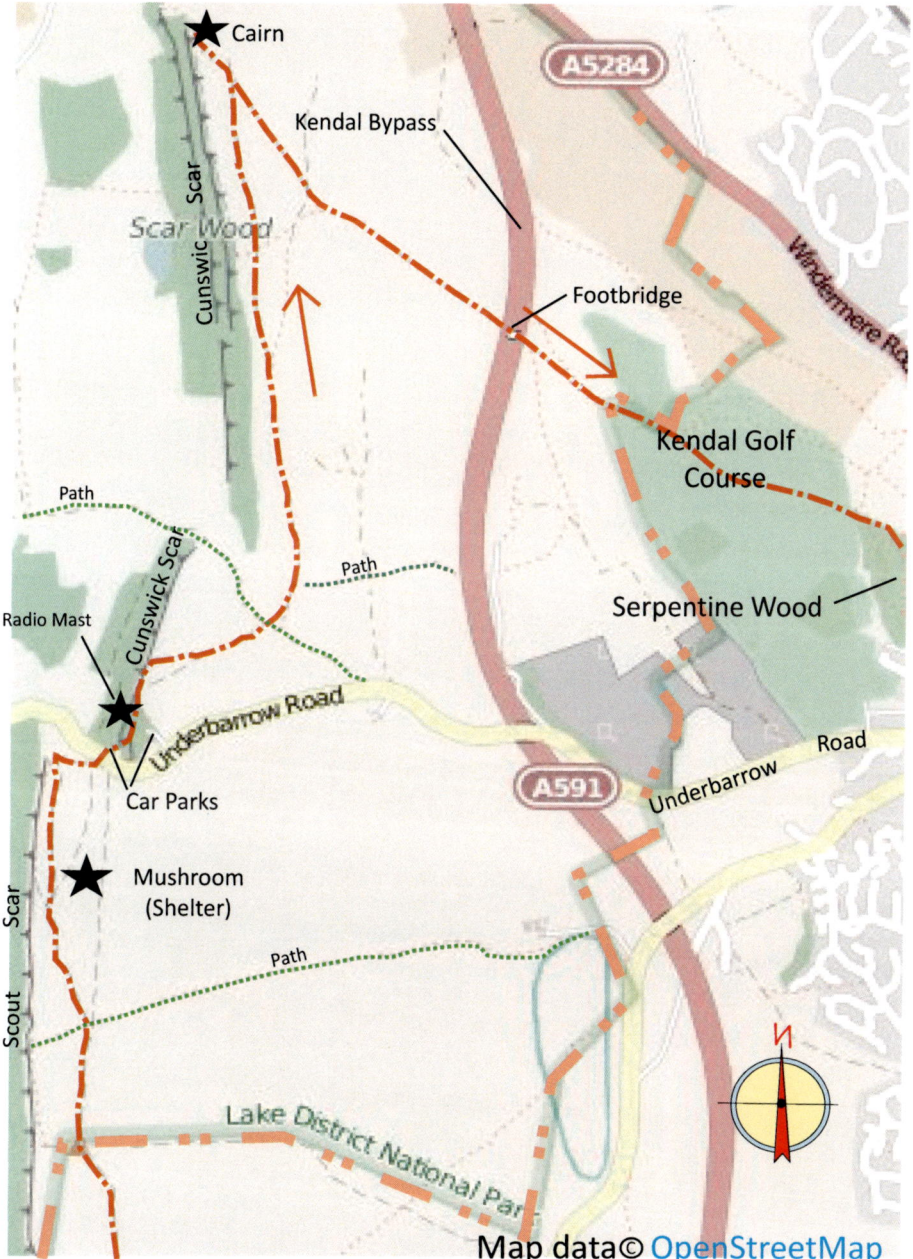

A5284

★ Cairn

Kendal Bypass

Windermere Rd

Scar Wood

Cunswick Scar

Footbridge

Kendal Golf Course

Path

Cunswick Scar

Path

Serpentine Wood

Radio Mast

Underbarrow Road

★

Car Parks

Underbarrow Road

A591

★ Mushroom (Shelter)

Scar

Path

Scout Scar

Lake District National Park

N

Map data© OpenStreetMap

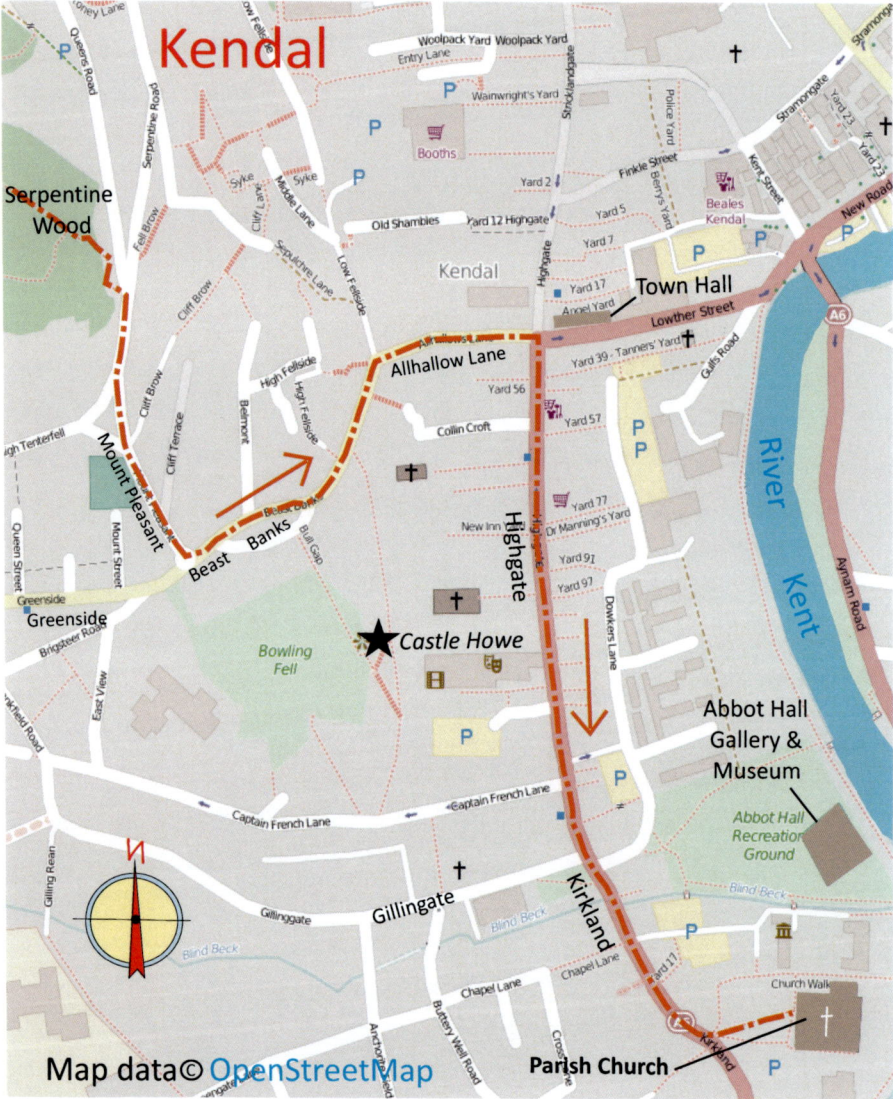

Kendal

Serpentine Wood

Queens Road

Serpentine Road

Honey Lane

Low Fellside

Sykue

Middle Lane

Cliff Brow

Fell Brow

Sepulchre Lane

Low Fellside

Cliff Brow

High Fellside

Belmont

Cliff Terrace

Cliff Brow

High Tenterfell

Mount Street

Queen Street

Mount Pleasant

Greenside

Brigsteer Road

East View

Anchefield Road

Gilling Rean

Beast Banks

Bull Gap

Butts Court

Greenside

Gillinggate

Gillingate

Blind Beck

Bowling Fell

★ **Castle Howe**

Captain French Lane

Captain French Lane

Chapel Lane

Buttery Well Road

Crossgate

Woolpack Yard Woolpack Yard

Entry Lane

Wainwright's Yard

Stricklandgate

Booths

Old Shambles

Yard 12 Highgate

Yard 2

Finkle Street

Berry's Yard

Yard 5

Yard 7

Kendal

Yard 17

Angel Yard

Allhallows Lane

Allhallow Lane

Yard 56

Collin Croft

New Inn Yard

Yard 57

Yard 77

Dr Manning's Yard

Yard 91

Yard 97

Highgate

Dowkers Lane

Town Hall

Lowther Street

Yard 39 Tanners' Yard

Gulfs Road

Police Yard

Stramongate

Kent Street

Yard 23

Yard 21

New Road

Beales Kendal

River Kent

A6

Aynam Road

Abbot Hall Recreation Ground

Abbot Hall Gallery & Museum

Blind Beck

Kirkland

Gillingate

Chapel Lane

Yard 17

Blind Beck

Church Walk

Kirkland

Parish Church

Map data© OpenStreetMap

Appendix B

Geology of Limestone Country

It is outside the scope of this guidebook to provide anything but a brief description of the main geological features found in limestone country. The following information may add to the enjoyment of the walk.

Limestone

Limestone is made of sediments which have settled on the seabed over millions of years. 300 million years ago most of the Yorkshire Dales and the south-eastern area of the Lake District were covered by a shallow tropical sea inhabited by millions of small filter feeding sea creatures. Sea water contains dissolved lime which the filter feeders extracted. The limey bones and shells of these creatures settled on the seabed and over time were compressed into limestone by the weight of mud (which turns to shale) and sand (which turns to sandstone) washed down by rivers into the sea. This cycle was repeated many times over millions of years as layers of limestone, shale and sandstone were formed.

Limestone Pavements

During the past two million years there have been at least three periods of glaciation affecting the Dales and the Cumbrian mountains and valleys, the last one beginning 80,000 years ago. As the ice advanced it stripped the softer rock and soil cover exposing the much harder limestone underneath leaving a flat surface of bear rock. Subsequent erosion of the pavement by wind, rainwater and frost action has created the present landscape. Hutton Roof Crags and Farleton Knott contain fine examples of limestone pavements.

Grikes

Grikes are the deep clefts that break up limestone pavements and give them a fractured appearance. Grikes have their own micro-climate and being moist and rich in lime and protected from nibbling sheep provide ideal conditions for plant growth - wood anemone, hart's-tongue fern, spleenwort, wild garlic and occasionally rare plants can be found.

Scars

Scars are made of a thick layer of shattered limestone which has been undercut by an advancing glacier. Twisleton Scars on the north side of Chapel-le-Dale and Raven Scar on the opposite side of the valley are classic examples of ice cutting deep into the limestone rock and creating a "U" shaped valley.

Geology of Limestone Country

Shake Holes

Shake holes (also called swallow holes) are a common feature of limestone country; they are funnel-shaped hollows formed where water has seeped into joints and cracks in the limestone rock below causing the limestone to dissolve and the ground above to collapse.

Caves, Potholes and Sinkholes

Caves, potholes and sinkholes are formed where slightly acidic surface water has flowed or percolated through cracks in the limestone rock until a drainage route is established enabling dissolved material to be washed away leaving a labyrinth of connecting passages and caves. Many potholes and sinkholes can be found along the Turbary Road above Masongill .

Erratics

Erratics are boulders standing on a narrow pedestal of rock above the limestone pavement. They are a relic of the last ice age having been plucked from their source, usually many miles away, by an advancing wall of ice and dumped in situ when the ice melted. Textbook examples of erratics can be found in the area above Proctor and Nappa Scars near Austwick where sandstone boulders rest on top of younger limestone.

Drumlins

Drumlins are smooth rounded hillocks, typically 500 metres long, and comprise of debris left in the final stages of glaciation. Their alignment indicates the direction in which the ice flowed. Many drumlins can be seen between Gargrave and Airton.

Appendix C

Useful Information

Tourist Information and Accommodation

Skipton Tourist Information Centre
Town Hall
High street
Skipton BD23 1AH
01756 792809

Settle Tourist Information
Town Hall
Settle BD24 9EJ
01729 825192

Ingleton Tourist Information
Ingleborough Community Centre
Main Street
Ingleton LA6 3HG
01542 41049

Kendal Tourist Information Centre
Made in Cumbria
25 Stramongate
Kendal LA9 4BH
01539 735891

Windermere Tourist Information Centre
Victoria Street
Windermere LA23 1AD
015394 46499

Malham National Park Centre
Malham
Skipton BD23 4DA
01729 833200

www.yorkshire.com
(The official visitor site for Yorkshire)

www.malhamdale.com

www.welcometoskipton.com

www.claphamyorkshire.co.uk

www.kirkbylonsdale.co.uk

www.visitlancashire.com
(For the Lune Valley)

(For the Lake District)
www.visitcumbria.com

www.exploresouthlakeland.co.uk

www.golakes.co.uk/kendal

Travel Information

www.nationalrail.co.uk
www.thetrainline.com
www.traveline.com
www.nationalexpress.com
www.dalesbus.org
www.kirkbylonsdalecoachhire.co.uk
(Travel information for the Yorkshire Dales)
www.stagecoachbus.com
(Travel information for Kendal and the Lake District)

Walking Associations

The Long Distance Walkers Association
www.ldwa.org.uk

Ramblers Association
www.ramblers.org.uk

YHA Youth Hostels
www.yha.org.uk
YHA on or close to the route
Malham and Ingleton
YHA some distance from the route
Arnside, Windermere and Ambleside

Mountain Rescue

Dial 999 and request *Police*

The Countryside Code

Enjoy the countryside and respect the local community and other people using the outdoors
Guard against all risk of fire
Leave all gates as you find them or follow instructions on signs
Keep your dogs under effective control. However, if cattle chase you and your dog, it is safer for you and your dog to let your dog off the lead
Always clean up after your dog "bag it and bin it"
Keep to public paths unless wider access is available under "open access land"
Use gates and stiles to cross fences, hedges and walls
Leave livestock, crops and machinery alone
Leave no trace of your visit and take your litter home
Help to keep all water clean
Protect wildlife, plants, trees and animals
Take special care on country roads
Make no unnecessary noise
Consider other people
Be safe - plan ahead and follow any signs

NB The above is an abbreviated version of the Countryside Code (October 2014 edition). The full code can be viewed or downloaded by visiting
https://www.gov.uk/government/publications/the-countryside-code

The Richmond Way

A walk from Lancaster to Richmond via the *Devil's Causeway*

John Coppack